Play ACOUSTIC GUITAR *in Minutes*

By Andrew DuBrock

ISBN 978-1-4584-2476-1

HAL•LEONARD®
CORPORATION
7777 W. BLUEMOUND RD. P.O. BOX 13819 MILWAUKEE, WI 53213

In Australia Contact:
Hal Leonard Australia Pty. Ltd.
4 Lentara Court
Cheltenham, Victoria, 3192 Australia
Email: ausadmin@halleonard.com.au

Visit Hal Leonard
www.hal

Table of Contents

Introduction

Anyone can play guitar! Whether you're five or 65, and whether you play other instruments or have never played any music in your life, all you need is a guitar and a few extra minutes each day. That's right—one of the most important parts of learning guitar is that you put in a few minutes *each* day, or as close to that as you can (if you can only do it three or four days a week, that's fine!). For your fingers to learn the muscle memory involved, it's much more efficient to play just a few minutes each day than it is to play several hours once a week. So therein lies the key. Be easy on yourself. Take it in small doses and put in the time that you have—whether that's five minutes or 45 minutes—and play your guitar as frequently as you can. Before you know it, you'll be finished with this book, working through another one, and playing songs with your friends.

Happy picking!

— *Andrew DuBrock*

About the Author

Andrew DuBrock is an independent music consultant who lives in Portland, Oregon. He has worked as an editor, transcriber, engraver, and author for Hal Leonard and served as Music Editor for *Acoustic Guitar*, *Strings*, and *Play Guitar!* magazines for seven years. A sampling of his instructional works include *Total Acoustic Guitar*, *Lennon and McCartney for Acoustic Guitar* (DVD), and *Rock/ Pop Guitar Songs for Dummies*. His independent acoustic pop/rock CD, *DuBrock*, can be found at **www.dubrock.net** and **www.cdbaby.com**.

To see more books and articles by Andrew DuBrock, or if you have comments or questions about this book, visit **www.andrewdubrock.com**

Acknowledgments

I'd like to thank my beautiful wife, Autumn, and my children, Leora and Will. for all their support during the writing of this book.

Thanks also to Jeff Schroedl and Hal Leonard for making this book possible.

Guitar Types

You can learn to play on any acoustic guitar. An "acoustic" guitar is any guitar that doesn't need amplification for you to play it. They have a hole on the front and are hollow inside (and usually at least a few inches deep). Classical (and some "folk") acoustic guitars use nylon strings, which are easy on the fingers, so they're easier to start with. However, many styles of popular music don't use nylon-string guitars as often as the steel-string acoustic guitar. While these are at first tougher on the fingers, they're by far the most common in popular music styles, including pop, rock, blue-grass/country, celtic, and modern folk. This book/DVD uses a steel-string acoustic guitar for the video portion, but any guitar you have or choose to play will work fine for strumming or fingerpicking. And if you only have access to an electric guitar, that will work fine for learning, too!

Guitar Anatomy

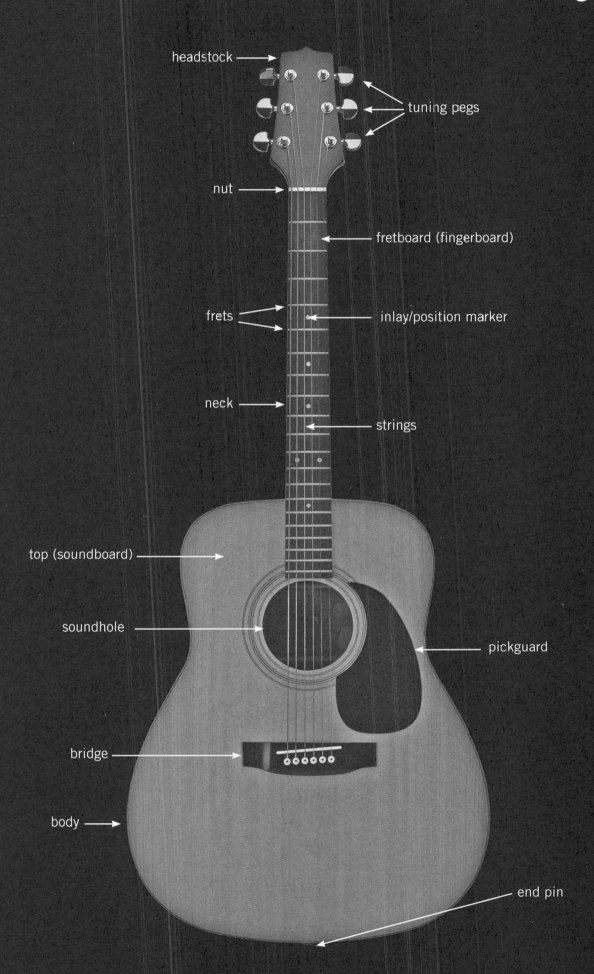

headstock

tuning pegs

nut

fretboard (fingerboard)

frets

inlay/position marker

neck

strings

top (soundboard)

soundhole

pickguard

bridge

body

end pin

SECTION I:
Getting Started

CHAPTER 1: GUITAR BASICS

Before we can play our guitars, we need to know how to hold them and tune them. Let's spend a few moments going over the basics.

Holding Your Guitar

You can hold your guitar in several ways. The most common way is to sit in an armless chair with your feet firmly planted on the ground. Place your guitar on your right leg with the neck of your guitar (the part with the frets) pointing to your left, as shown in the following picture.

ARE YOU A LEFTY?

If you're left handed, hold your guitar in a mirror image of the previous picture. Place the guitar on your *left* leg (instead of your right), with the neck of your guitar (the part with the frets) pointing to your right.

Classical guitarists use a footstool under their left foot and place their guitar on their *left* leg. The footstool angles the guitar back towards your left hand, making it easier to play notes on the fretboard. It's less common for folk, rock, or singer-songwriters to play like this, but it's worth trying out, especially if you find it more difficult to play without a footstool. You should hold the guitar in whatever way works best for you.

If you want to play standing up, use a strap and adjust it so that the guitar naturally falls where your hands have easy access to it.

HOW HIGH SHOULD I ADJUST MY STRAP?

You have the best access to your guitar when it's rather high—up close to your chest. However, this can look a little awkward, and some rockers like to strap their guitars extremely low because it looks "cool." Unfortunately, your guitar is much harder to play when it's down low. A good compromise is to have your guitar somewhere in the middle, as shown in the picture.

Holding the Pick

Hold the pick between your thumb and index finger by following these steps: First, relax your hand and let the fingers naturally curl inwards. Then—using this naturally relaxed position—place the pick between your thumb and index finger and apply just enough pressure to hold it in place. Applying too much pressure with your thumb can tire your thumb out *and* cause you to have a harder time strumming the guitar naturally. (Of course, you'll need to keep enough pressure on the pick so that it doesn't fall out of your hand when you strum!)

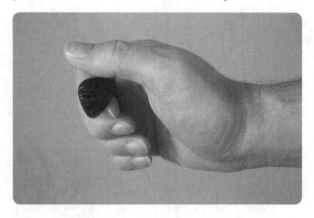

Relax your hand, turn it sideways to provide a shelf for the pick, and place the pick on your index finger.

Close your thumb on the pick, applying just enough pressure to hold it in place for strumming.

Fret-Hand Fingers

When we play guitar, we use all four fingers of our fretting hand. Your index finger is commonly called your "first finger," with your middle, ring, and pinky fingers called the "second," "third," and "fourth" fingers, respectively.

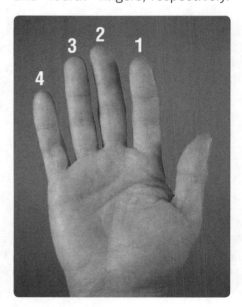

In the music, Arabic numerals near the notes often show you which fingers to use. Notice how these numbers are placed near the notes in the music staff—not near the fret numbers in the tablature staff:

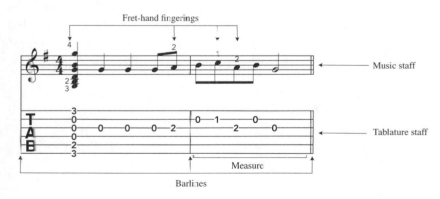

In the previous example, the vertical lines are called barlines, and the space between each pair of barlines is called a measure. (*For more information on understanding the music, see "Reading Music" in the* Appendix).

When you play chords and notes on your guitar, plant the thumb of your fretting hand on the back of the guitar's neck, as shown in the picture. While guitarists occasionally slide the neck of the guitar into the space between the thumb and fingers, it's best to try and keep your thumb on the back of the neck as much as possible, since it gives you more support for pressing down the strings and gives your fingers more mobility to move freely around your guitar's fretboard.

Guitar Strings

The six strings on your guitar are labeled from the highest string to the lowest string, as shown here.

1 = high E string
2 = B string
3 = G string
4 = D string
5 = A string
6 = low E string

When you hold the guitar on your lap, notice that the highest-sounding string (the high E string) ends up closest to the ground, while the lowest-sounding string (the low E string) is the closest to the ceiling. This often confuses guitarists, since the highest string is "on the bottom" and the lowest string is "on the top." Try to remember that the strings are named that way because of the pitch they produce—not their geographical location while in playing position.

Tuning Your Guitar

Tune your guitar's strings to the notes E–A–D–G–B–E, from low to high (remember: the lowest string is the biggest one; the one on *top* when you hold your guitar on your lap). The easiest way to tune your guitar is to use an electronic tuner. For each string you tune, pluck the string and then twist the knob on the headstock that's attached to that string until the tuner indicates it's in tune. If you get your low E string in tune by using a tuner or matching another instrument's E note, you can tune your guitar yourself:

1. Once your sixth string is in tune, tune your fifth string by matching it to the fifth fret of the sixth string.

2. Then tune the fourth string by matching it to the fifth fret of the fifth string.

3. Next, tune your third string by matching it to the fifth fret of the fourth string.

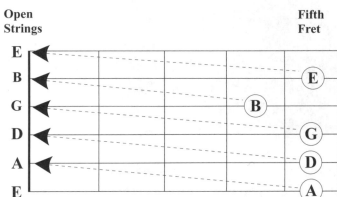

4. Then tune your second string by matching it to the *fourth* fret of the third string.

5. Finally, tune your first string by matching it to the fifth fret of the second string.

CHAPTER 2: YOUR FIRST CHORDS AND STRUMS

If you simply strum through the open strings of your guitar, it doesn't sound all that great. So before we start strumming anything, we have to learn how to fret a chord shape that sounds good when we strum through the strings. We'll start out with a D chord.

THE D CHORD

Place your index finger behind the second fret of the third string, your ring finger behind third fret of the second string, and your middle finger behind the second fret of the first string.

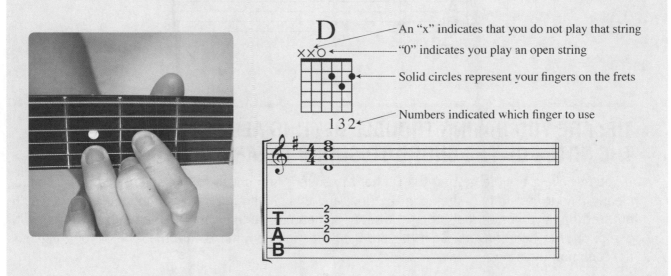

An "x" indicates that you do not play that string

"0" indicates you play an open string

Solid circles represent your fingers on the frets

Numbers indicated which finger to use

The picture and chord grid graphic above both represent the same thing, but notice how the chord grid graphic is oriented in a different way. The picture shows what it looks like when you're standing in front of someone playing the D chord on the guitar. The strings in the picture are horizontal (parallel to the floor). But the chord grid shows how the chord shape looks on a vertically oriented guitar. Imagine the guitar is in a stand with its strings pointing vertically up and down (perpendicular to the floor). To match up the picture and the graphic, you'll have to imagine one or the other rotating 90° to match the other. This small discrepancy between the graphic and picture often creates a lot of confusion, so take a close look at the two and make sure you can see how they both relate to each other before moving on.

Once you have your fingers in place for the D chord, you're ready to test whether you have the strings fretted properly by plucking each string one at a time with the pick and making sure that each note sounds clearly. For the D chord, we strum through the first four strings *only*. (Remember: the top four strings are the ones closer to the floor.) Start on the fourth string (D) and pluck each of the four strings as you move your arm down towards the floor. If you hear any buzzing as you pluck a string, adjust your fretting finger until the note sounds clear. To help eliminate buzzing, position your fretting fingers close to the frets they are immediately behind. Once all of the notes are clear, strum all the way through the chord. (If you're still having problems getting the chord to sound, see the nearby "tip.")

Now let's practice that D chord several times. Strum the chord and count the beats—"one, two, three, four"—then strum the chord again for four more beats. As you can see in the following music, whole notes (those empty circles) each get four beats. The repeat signs (double bar with one thick and one thin line next to two dots) indicate you should repeat everything between the signs. (*For more information on understanding the music, see "Reading Music" in the* Appendix.) We're going to use downstrokes for these strums; start with your arm above the strings and then strum downwards, towards the floor, through the four strings of the D chord. The downstroke symbol is shown between the notation and tablature and it looks like this: ⊓

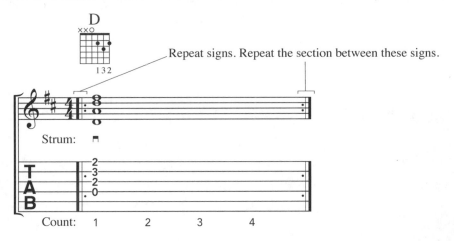

Repeat signs. Repeat the section between these signs.

Strum: ⊓

Count: 1   2   3   4

TIP: ARE YOU HAVING TROUBLE GETTING ALL THE NOTES OF THE CHORD TO SOUND CLEARLY?

If you're having trouble getting the D chord to sound, first check to make sure each note sounds clearly. The lowest note is the open D string, and this should naturally sound clearly, since you're not fretting anything on that string. However, sometimes we inadvertantly dampen this string with one of our fret-hand fingers. So if this string sounds muffled, make sure that one of your fingers is not touching the string.

For each of the other three strings in the chord, make sure you press down firmly enough so that the note sounds clearly when you pluck it. But don't press *too hard!* It's a combination of pressing and finger placement. The closer you are to the frets, the less pressure you need to apply to the string. So if the string buzzes, try moving your finger a little closer to the fret. The pictures below show the fingers right behind the frets where it's easier to hold down the strings (below, left) as well as the fingers in the middle of the frets where you'll need to apply a little more pressure (below, right).

Place your fingers directly behind each fret, like this.

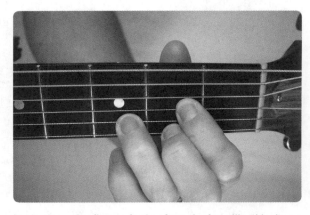

Don't place your fingers farther from the frets like this; it can cause extra buzz.

Since it's easier to press the strings down when you're right behind them, it's a good idea to try and keep your fingers as close to the frets as possible. But when you're playing chords with several fingers, as we are here, it's not always possible to fret *every* note right behind the fret, because some chord shapes make it hard to do that (and some hand sizes do too!). So don't worry too much about being *right* behind the fret for everything. Instead, concentrate on being close to the frets and focus on making the chords sound clean and clear. If there's buzzing, then you can try to read-just your finger placement, but if the chord sounds good, then you're doing fine!

One final note: when you start playing guitar, it's harder to press down the strings since you don't have callouses. This also means that if you play a lot, the pads of your fingers will likely be sore. But this will all be gone before long! You should start developing callouses on your fingers within a few weeks, and then you'll be able to play longer and fret chords a little more easily.

First Strum: Quarter-Note Strum Pattern

Our first strum pattern uses *quarter notes*. Quarter notes each get one beat, so when you count along ("one, two, three, four"), that means you'll strum on every beat—every time you say a number.

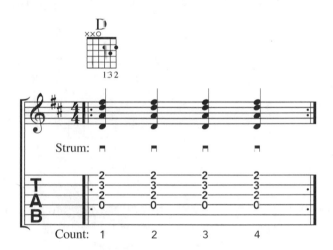

The tricky part here is that you have to get your pick back up to start the next strum every beat and, since we don't strum every string on a D chord, a bit of precision is required. If you have trouble doing this, all you need to do is slow down and count your beats at a slow enough pace that you *can* get your pick up to the right place in time for the next beat. If you have a metronome, this a great time to use it. Set it at a slow pace and play a strum for each click of the metronome. Then, as you get more comfortable strumming each beat, you can increase the tempo a couple of clicks, play through it again until you're comfortable at the slightly quicker pace, and keep gradually increasing the speed until you can play the strums at a moderate tempo (100–120 beats per minute [bpm]).

Now that you can play a strum pattern, you have all the tools to play a song! There are plenty of songs you can play that use just one chord. For instance, let's try "Row, Row, Row Your Boat" using a D chord and playing our quarter-note strum pattern.

This is a big step to take: trying out our new strum pattern *and* singing at the same time. So pat yourself on the back if you can pull it off! But don't worry if you're having a little trouble; most everyone does at this point. One way to get yourself comfortable singing and playing a song is to slow your strums down until you're comfortable singing along. Let's go back to our whole-note strum pattern and try this. Now, all you have to do is strum every four or five words (look at the music to see exactly where).

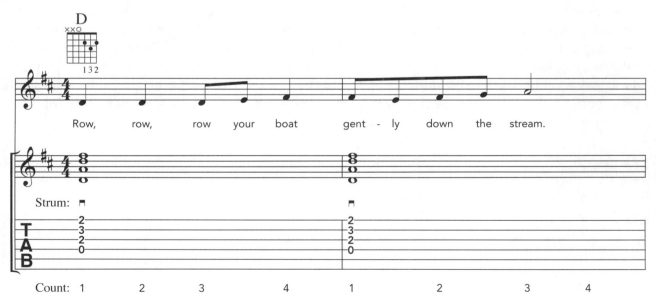

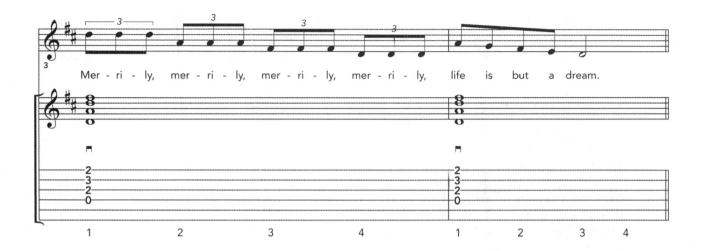

Since you can't count along as you sing, it may help if you tap your foot on every beat or play along to a metronome. Once you're comfortable playing through the song with a whole-note strum pattern, try going back to quarter-note strums. And remember to play it at a slow enough speed that you can sing and play each strum cleanly and in rhythm. If you have trouble, slow things down to a speed at which you *can* perform the song, and gradually speed it up to performance tempo a few metronome clicks at a time.

THE A CHORD

To play an A chord, you'll fret three strings *all* in the second-fret space. Place your index, middle, and ring fingers on the fourth, third, and second strings, respectively (all behind the second fret). This is how an A chord looks:

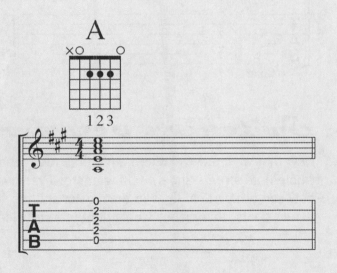

For the A chord, we strum through *five* of the strings (again, the five closest to the floor). Test whether you have the strings fretted properly for the A chord by plucking each string one at a time, making sure that each note sounds clear. If you hear buzzing, adjust your fretting finger until you get a clear sound.

The previous fingering is just one way you can fret an A chord. Some players like to swap strings with their index and middle fingers (see below), which can make changing between the A chord and some other chords a little easier. Try both ways and use the fingering you find most comfortable:

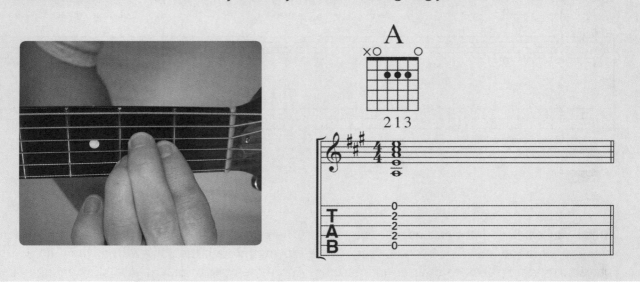

Once you have the A chord under your fingers, first practice it with a whole-note strum pattern, then try it with a quarter-note strum.

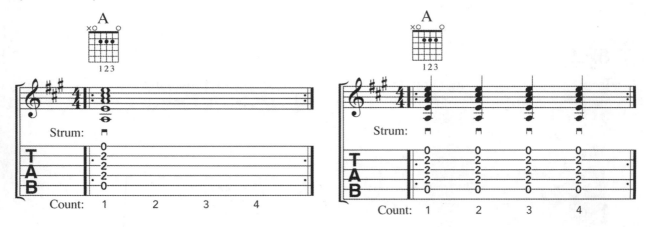

Switching Between Chords

Now that we know two chords, it's time to practice switching between them. Let's start by playing whole-note strums and switching chords every two measures. (Remember: a *measure* is the space between two vertical lines in the music, and the vertical lines are called *barlines*.) Since a measure is four beats, this means we'll count to four twice before changing chords.

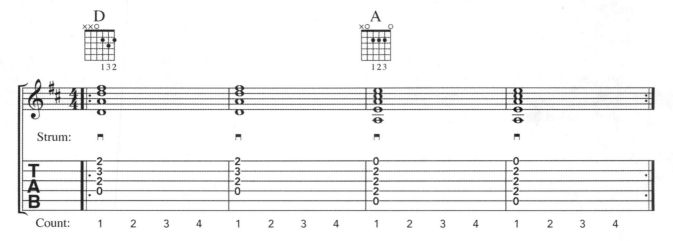

Don't worry if you have trouble making the switch; this can take a while for most people to get comfortable with. One trick that's good to know is that you can't possibly move your fretting hand *exactly at the same time* as your picking hand strums. That means you'll need to get that fretting hand in place *before* the strum. So, any time after you count beat "four," you can start moving those fretting fingers into place for the next chord.

Remember that you can slow down the tempo until you're able to make the switch in rhythm. It's important that you're able to make the switch *in time*—meaning that you can make the switch without your counting slowing down right before the switch and then speeding up again after. That's because you need to learn how to play steady rhythms or else you'll have trouble playing with other people (imagine trying to play with someone who's always speeding up and slowing down!).

Once you're comfortable switching between chords every two measures, let's try switching between chords *every* measure:

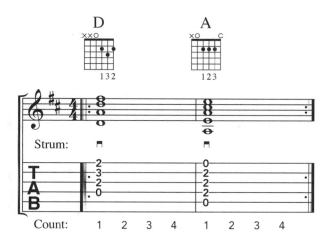

TIP: USE GUIDE FINGERS

When switching between chords, it's helpful to find fingers that you can use as guides. For instance, when you switch between the D and A chords, there are several different fingers you can use as guides, depending on which A chord fingering you use. If you use the first A chord fingering shown (with your index, middle, and ring fingers all in a row), notice how your ring finger frets notes on the second string for *both* the A and D chords; it holds down the second fret for the A chord and the third fret for the D chord. You can use this finger as a guide by leaving it on the string when you switch chords. Start with the D chord and, as you lift your other fingers off of the strings to switch to the A chord, let this ring finger slide down a fret, popping you into position for the A chord, where you simply put your other two fingers in place. (You can release pressure just a little for the guide finger, but not so much that you can't feel the strings and fret; otherwise it won't act as a guide.)

When you switch from the A chord back to the D chord, use that ring finger as a guide in the same way: lift the other fingers off the strings and slide the ring finger *up* a fret, then pop your other fingers in place for the D chord.

Now let's try switching between chords using our quarter-note strum pattern:

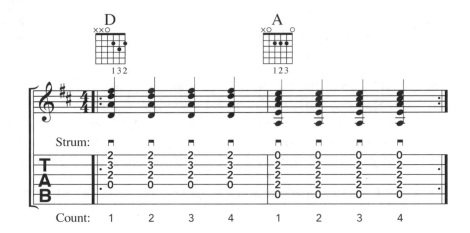

Now that you're playing strums on every beat, you have a little less time to move those fret-hand fingers into place for the chord change, but you still *do* have some time. You can visualize it this way: your strumming hand should be moving steadily down and up (always moving down when you count each beat). As your strumming hand moves *up*, it's not strumming the strings, and you can start moving those fret-hand fingers at this point. This should give you enough time to get those fingers into place for the next chord.

We'll finish this chapter with another song. "Tom Dooley" uses two chords (D and A), switching back and forth once. Let's start by playing it with our whole-note strum pattern.

TOM DOOLEY

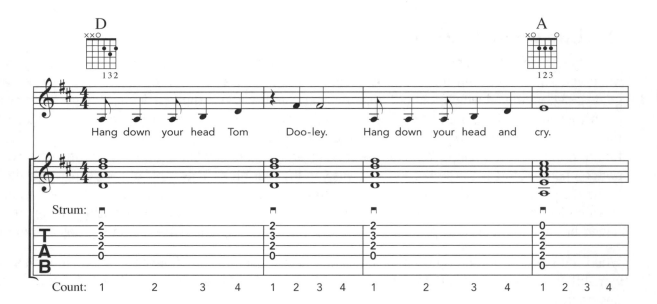

Once you're comfortable with this, you can try the song using our quarter-note strum pattern. Try both ways and see which way you like better. Sometimes a simpler strum pattern actually sounds better, but it's up to you to choose which way you like best.

TOM DOOLEY

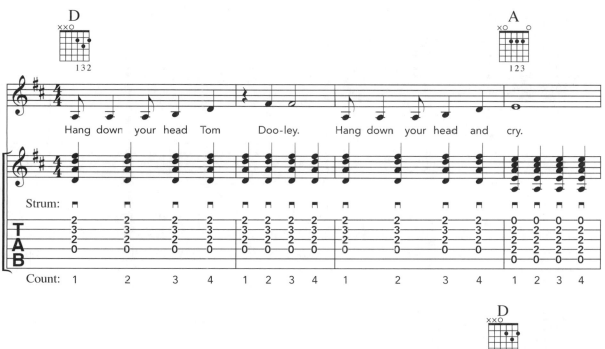

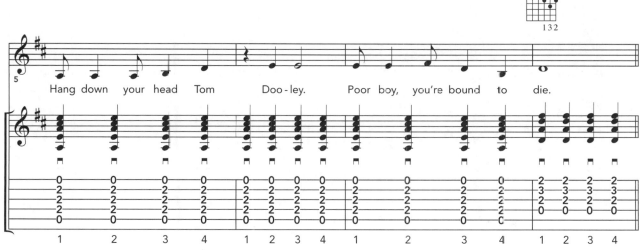

CHAPTER 3: THE I–IV–V PROGRESSION

Musicians often use numbers to help communicate chord progressions to each other (a *chord progression* is any series of chords). When they use those numbers, each number corresponds to a chord. If you've ever heard someone say "It's a I–IV–V progression in E," they're telling someone else what chord progression to play in this universal language of chords and numbers. Before we get into what these numbers mean, let's learn a few more chords. (Right now, we only know two chords, but we'll need to know at least three to play a I–IV–V progression.)

THE G CHORD

Get your fretting hand in place for a G chord by placing your ring, middle, and pinky fingers on the sixth, fifth, and first strings, respectively. Your ring and pinky fingers both sit in the third-fret space, while your middle finger sits in the second-fret space. This is how a G chord looks:

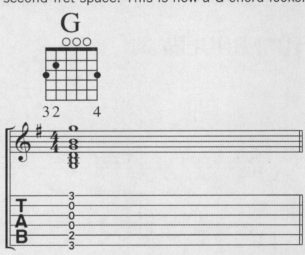

We get to strum through all six strings of our G chord (our first chord where we get to do this!). This makes strumming the chord a bit easier than the D or A chords. If you have small hands or have trouble fretting a G chord with the above fingering, following are several alternate fingerings you can try:

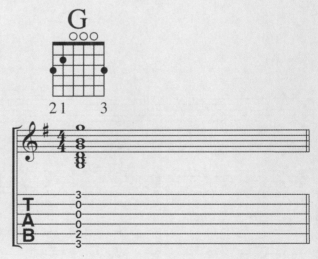

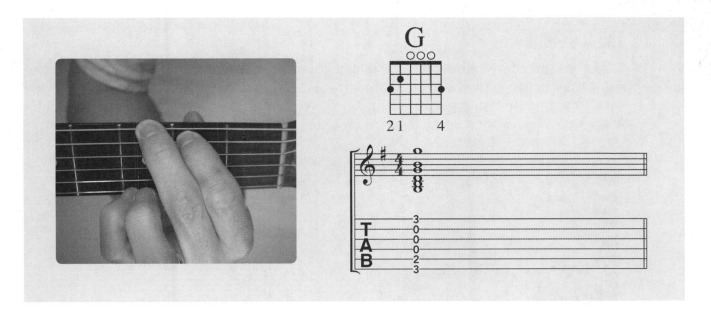

Once you have the G chord under your fingers, practice strumming it for a while using whole notes and quarter notes, then try changing between the G and D chords:

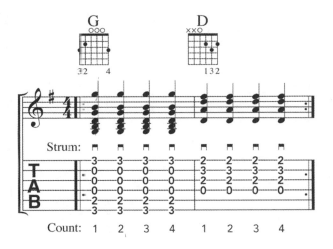

Whenever you learn a new chord, it's a good idea to practice changing between that chord and as many other chords as you can. So let's practice changing between the G and A chords, as well.

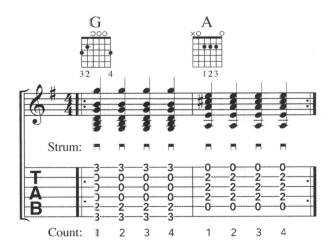

THE C CHORD

To play a C chord, place your ring, middle, and index fingers on the fifth, fourth, and second strings, respectively. For this chord, each finger will lie in a different fret space. Your ring finger sits in the third-fret space, your middle finger sits in the second-fret space, and your index finger sits in the first-fret space. This is how a C chord looks:

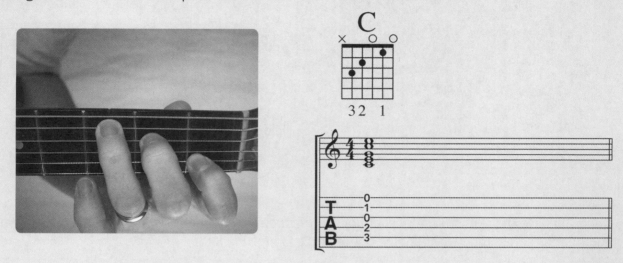

Again, test whether you have the strings fretted properly for the C chord by plucking each string one at a time, making sure that each note sounds clear.

Once you're comfortable with the C chord, practice changing between C and each of the other chords we've learned so far. Let's start with C–G (chord progressions are often written as chord symbols with dashes between them):

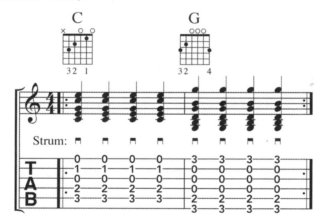

Next, try changing between C and D. Then try C–A, which is a little different, but still a nice chord change:

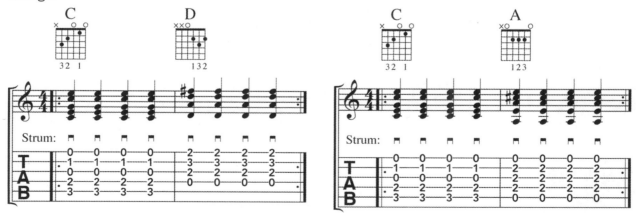

Your First I–IV–V Progression

The I–IV–V chord progression is one of the most popular progressions in pop and rock music. We have enough chords now to play a I–IV–V chord progression in the key of G. When we say we're "in the key of G," that means that the G chord sounds like "home"—it's the chord that we want to resolve to and is often the starting and/or ending chord of a song. Notice that the G chord in the following progression is labelled as the I chord and the C and D chords are labelled IV and V, respectively. (*To understand how they get this name, see the nearby* Tip *as well as the* Appendix— *especially the "Major Scale and Major Key Chord Functions" section.*)

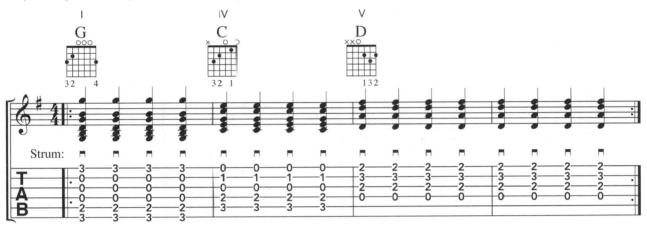

Do you recognize this progression? Countless rock songs use it, including "Twist and Shout," which was made famous by the Beatles in the early 1960s, and "La Bamba," popularized by Ritchie Valens in the late 1950s. Notice that we play the G and C chords for one measure, but we play the D chord for *two* measures. Chord progressions often (though not always) fall easily into an even number of measures—like the four measures here. Try playing the same progression with only one measure for the D chord, and notice how it sounds a little cut off:

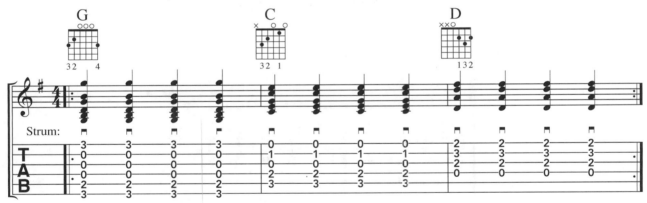

TIP: WHY IS IT CALLED A I–IV–V PROGRESSION?

The chords in any key all have a relationship to each other. We're in the key of G here, so we call G the I chord, and everything else is in relation to that G chord. How do we know where the IV chord is? We count up four notes from G to get there, starting with G as the first number. The musical alphabet only uses the notes A through G, after which point they simply start over again. So, if we start from G, we count G (1), A (2), B (3), C (4). C is the fourth note we reach, so C is the IV chord. What's the V chord? Let's count up from G to the fifth degree: G (1), A (2), B (3), C (4), D (5). So D is the V chord.

This gets slightly more complicated when you move to other keys, because many keys use sharped (♯) and flatted (♭) notes, but we're not going to worry about that yet. If you're really curious about this, see the *Appendix* section on "Chord Theory" and "Major Scale and Major Key Chord Functions."

Eighth-Note Strums

Now let's try some eighth-note strums. An *eighth note* has only half the value of a quarter note. That means we're going to strum twice as many times as we do for quarter-note strums. We still move our arm up and down at exactly the same speed, but now we'll start using *upstrokes.* Before, we were only playing *downstrokes*—a motion that starts with our arm above the strings and continues down toward the floor. But as we bring our arm back up, we can strum the strings again. Let's try this on a G chord. If you count along, every time you say a number, you should be playing a downstroke, and each upstroke will fall between your counts. (An upstroke is shown with a symbol that looks like a "V" between the notation and tablature.)

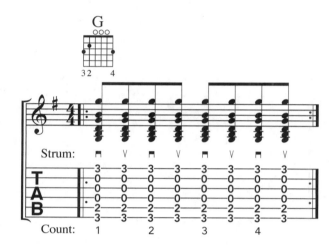

Make sure that you're strumming with a steady up-and-down motion. It's like walking; once you're comfortable with it, you won't have to think about it at all. If you want to count along to the eighth notes, add an "and" between each number (1-and, 2-and, 3-and, 4-and). With this counting method, every downstroke will fall on a number, and every upstroke will fall on an "and."

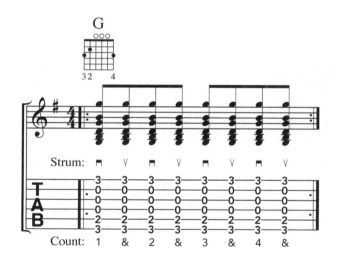

Once you're comfortable with upstrokes, let's try our I–IV–V chord progression with our new strum pattern. Make sure to slow this down if you need to so that you can play the chord changes in time (without slowing down for the change and speeding up again).

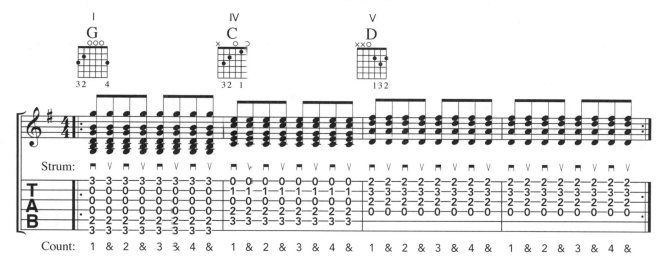

TIP: CHORD CHANGING TRICK

Here's a trick *every* guitarist uses to make their chord changes easier—they start switching chords a little early and strum the open strings while they get their fingers into place. If you strum the open strings for only the last eighth note of a chord, it doesn't sound too bad. This gives your fingers more time to get into place for the next chord. Listen closely to some of your favorite songs, and you'll be surprised at how often this happens. Here's how it sounds in our I–IV–V progression:

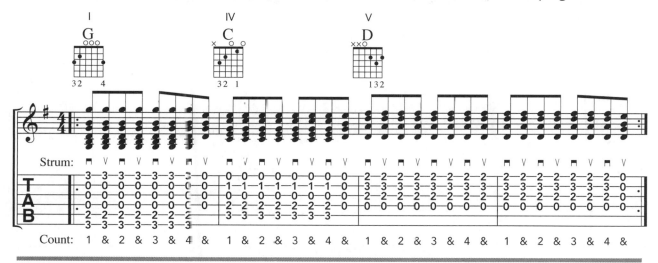

We'll finish this chapter by learning a song. "Shake It Up, Now," on the following page, uses a I–IV–V progression similar to the classic "Twist and Shout" sound. This is a great practice for switching between our G, C, and D chords while we play a song. If you have trouble putting together the strumming, chord changes, and singing, try practicing each on their own until you can play and sing each part by memory. Then, put the vocal and guitar part back together at a very slow tempo (and play with a metronome, if you have one!). Once you can play them together at a slow tempo, gradually increase your speed until you can play it at the pace you want.

TIP: DOTTED NOTES

If you look at the vocal part in measure 6, you'll see a dot after the note (above the word "oh"). A dot adds half a note's value to itself. In this case, the dot is behind a half note, which normally has two beats, but the dot adds half that value to it (one more beat) so the dotted half note equals *three* beats. If you have a dotted quarter note, it equals one-and-one-half beats (or the value of three eighth notes).

SHAKE IT UP, NOW

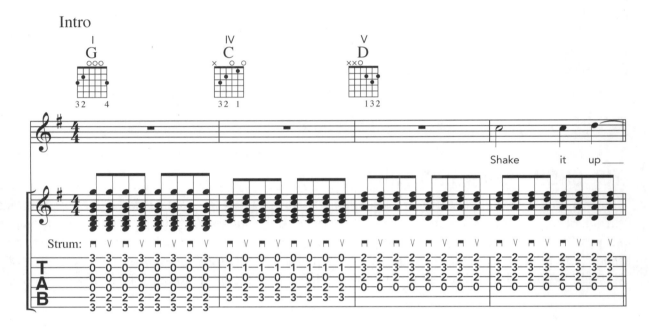

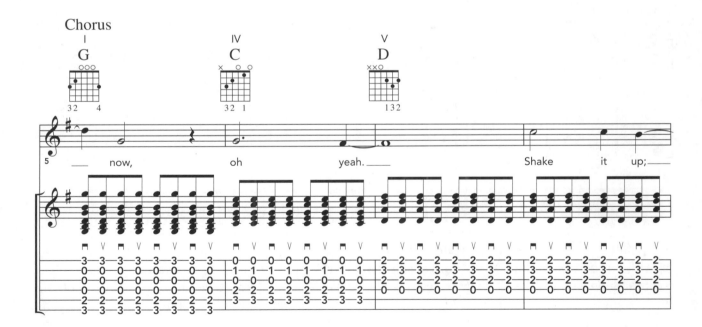

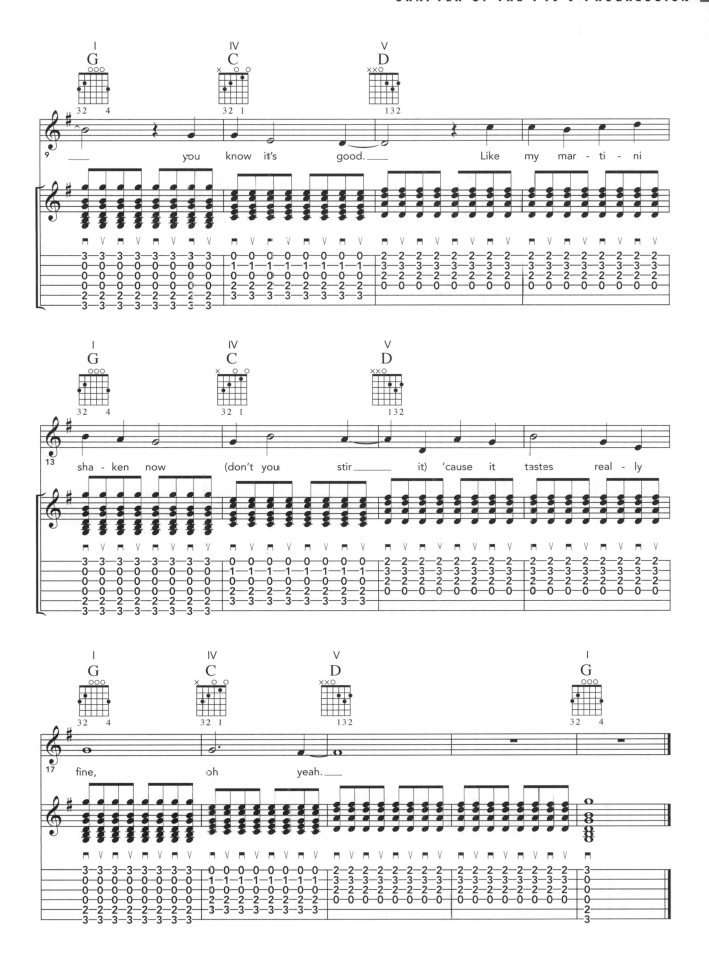

CHAPTER 4: EXPANDING YOUR STRUMS

Your rhythm can sound a little monotonous when you're just strumming steady quarter notes or eighth notes, so let's try putting these two together. We'll start out with a pattern that uses a quarter note followed by six eighth notes. First, practice it on one chord. We'll try it with a G chord here:

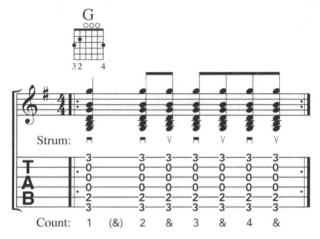

When you're mixing quarter notes and eighth notes, it can be easier to lose the rhythm than when you're playing only quarter notes or eighth notes. One way to help keep a steady rhythm going is to *count* all of the eighth-note subdivisions, even though you're not playing them all. Look at the previous example and notice the silent (parenthesized) "and" after the first downstroke. If you count this "and" as your pick moves back up (or tap your foot), you'll be counting out a steady rhythm while you strum. Now try playing our I–IV–V chord progression in the key of G using our new strum pattern:

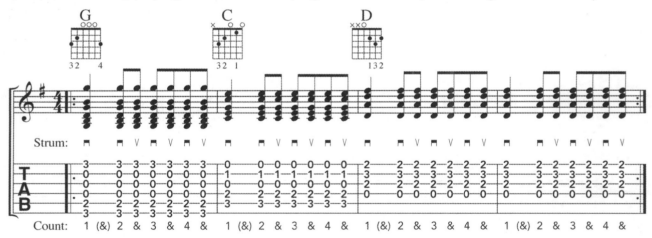

TIP: PENDULUM STRUMMING

When you start mixing up eighth notes and quarter notes in your strum patterns, it may throw your rhythm off if you think too much about the downstrokes and upstrokes. The most important thing is to keep your strumming arm moving constantly up and down in a steady motion. Just as you don't have uneven strides when you're running or walking, you don't have a quick downstroke and a long upstroke; the downstrokes and upstrokes are all the same, and your arm moves naturally like a pendulum going back and forth. For eighth-note strums, your arm will connect with the strings on both the downstrokes and upstrokes. And for the quarter-note strums, you'll strum down and then come up without connecting with the strings (an "air strum"). It all comes back to keeping your arm moving in a steady down-and-up motion, so remember to relax and feel the groove—the rhythm of your arm's steady motion.

You can mix eighth notes and quarter notes up in many different combinations. Let's try one that uses a quarter note followed by two eighth notes, then repeats that combination for the second half of the measure, like this:

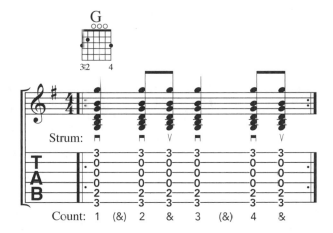

Remember to count all of those eighth-note subdivisions—even the silent ones, which are shown under the tablature staff. And don't forget to try this out with our I–IV–V chord progression:

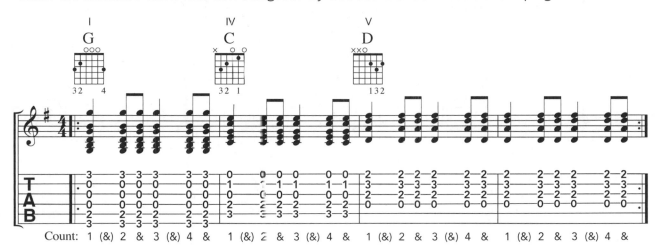

Now it's your turn! Come up with a few of your own strumming patterns. We've been using strumming patterns that repeat every measure, but you can spread them out over several measures if you want to. Within the context of a song, this can sound great, too. Here's one to get you started. This one takes the two strum patterns from this chapter and pastes then together into one longer pattern:

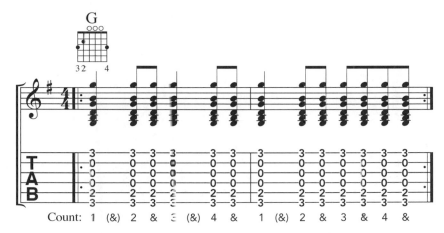

I–IV–V in the Key of D

So far, we've played our I–IV–V progression in the key of G. But you can play this same chord progression in any other key, as well. (When we play in a different key, that means that a different chord will be the I or "home" chord.) Let's try it in the key of D. In the key of D, we call D the I chord because it sounds like "home." Now let's just count up the letters to find the IV and V chords. To get the IV chord, we count up to the fourth degree—D (1), E (2), F♯ (3), G (4)—so G is the IV chord. (*If you want to know why we counted through F♯—instead of just F—see the nearby Tip and the* Appendix). To get the V chord, let's count up to the fifth degree: D (1), E (2), F♯ (3), G (4), A (5). So A is our V chord. Now let's plug these chords into the progression using one of our mixed patterns:

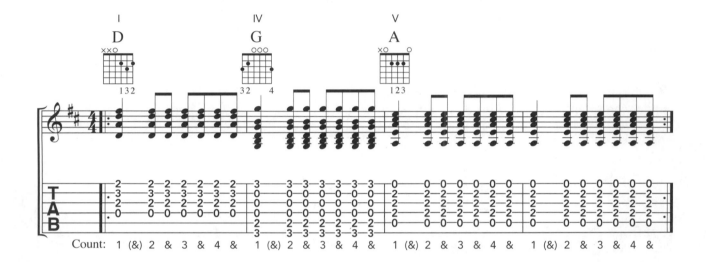

Count: 1 (&) 2 & 3 & 4 &   1 (&) 2 & 3 & 4 &   1 (&) 2 & 3 & 4 &   1 (&) 2 & 3 & 4 &

TIP: WHY ARE THERE SHARPED OR FLATTED NOTES?

When we counted up from D to get our IV and V chords in the key of D, we used F♯ instead of F. That's because F♯ is in the D major scale. Whenever we want to find the IV or V chords in any key, we're actually counting up that key's major scale. So, when you want to find the IV and V chords in the key of C, you start from C and count up using the C major scale; in the key of A, you start on A and count up the A major scale, etc. Each one of these major scales uses different notes, and some of them use sharps while others use flats. To understand *which* notes belong to any major scale, you need to learn how to build major scales. You can learn about this in the *Appendix* and from Hal Leonard's book *Music Theory for Guitarists*.

THE E CHORD

Get your fretting hand in place for an E chord by placing your middle, ring, and index fingers on the fifth, fourth, and third strings, respectively. Your ring and middle fingers both sit in the second-fret space, while your index finger sits in the first-fret space. This is how an E chord looks:

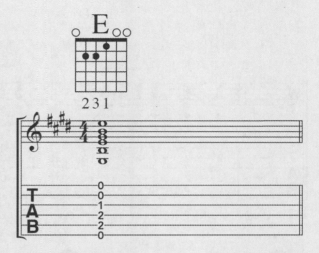

Just as you did with the previous chords, test whether you have the strings fretted properly for the E chord by plucking each string one at a time with your thumb or a finger, making sure that each note sounds clear.

I–IV–V in the Key of A

Now that we know how to play an E chord, we can play a I–IV–V progression in the key of A. As you might expect, the I chord in the key of A is A. To find the IV and V chords, we'll simply count up the scale. (Before we count, I'll mention that the A major scale uses three sharped notes: C♯, F♯, and G♯. If you want to know more about the theory behind this, see the *Appendix*.) To get to the IV chord, let's count up from A: A (1), B (2), C♯ (3), D (4). So, D is our IV chord. And the V chord?: A (1), B (2), C♯ (3), D (4), E (5). So E is our V chord. That means our I–IV–V progression in the key of A is A–D–E:

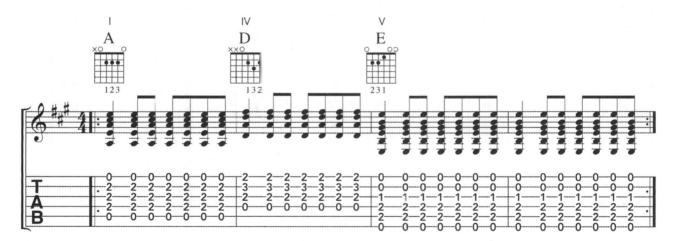

Let's try that again with a new strum pattern. This time we'll play two quarter notes followed by four eighth notes in each measure. Remember to count along at first, to keep yourself playing steady rhythms. And make sure you continue to strum each quarter note with a downstroke and each pair of eighth notes with a pair of downstrokes and upstrokes:

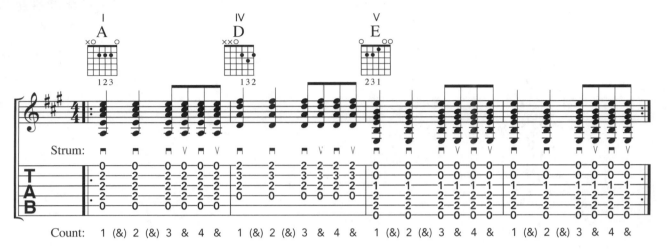

Syncopated Strumming

Now it's time for us to learn a trick that will help us make our strums much funkier, while also allowing us to create countless more patterns. The trick involves adding *syncopation* into our strumming patterns. Syncopation basically means that you accent weak beats. The strongest beats happen on beats 1 and 3, so if you highlight beats 2 and 4, you're already playing a syncopated pattern. To really hear (and feel) how this works, let's start off by playing beat 1, but then we'll play only beats two and four for several measures. Set yourself up with a metronome or tap your foot as you play, and you'll really hear the syncopation if you're able to set beat 1 (and even beat 3) to be louder than the other beats. We'll try this on an E chord, and we'll use all downstrokes, since we're only playing on the beats (those curvy lines between notes are called *ties*; see the nearby "Tip" for an explanation):

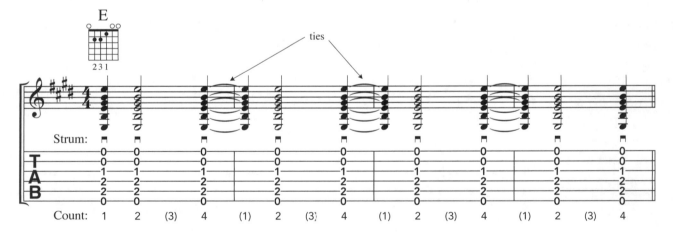

TIP: TIES

Ties are curved lines that look like sideways parentheses. Their function is to rhythmically join notes together. Any time you see a tie, you only pluck the first note, and the tied note simply extends that note across a beat or a barline.

Don't worry if you have trouble with this. It's really just an exercise to help you hear basic syncopation. Most syncopation in strum patterns actually uses shorter durations than this—like eighth notes, for instance. To play eighth-note syncopation, all you have to do is leave out one of the beats (1, 2, 3, 4). This naturally puts a little more emphasis on one of the upstroke "ands," creating syncopation. Since we play all downstrokes on beats 1–4, we simply leave out one of our downstrokes. Let's leave out beat 3 to see how this kind of syncopation sounds:

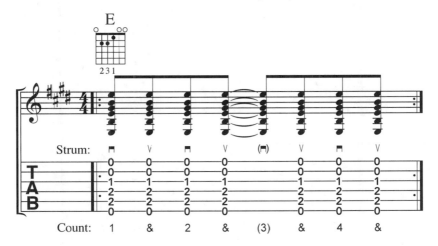

Remember that, even though you're not playing a downstroke on beat 3, you still need to keep your arm moving. As your arm moves down on beat 3, just keep it away from the strings so it doesn't create a strum.

Let's try syncopating a different place in our strum pattern. This time, let's leave out the downstroke on beat 2:

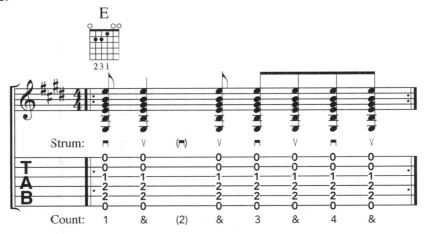

And we can add syncopation in more than one place, as well. Here, let's leave out the downstrokes on *both* beats 2 and 3:

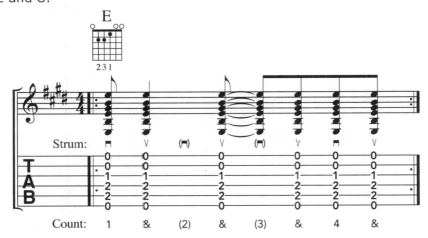

It's syncopation like this that gives songs their own "groove." For instance, let's make a two-measure strum pattern with syncopation using an A chord. (A one-measure pattern would work fine, too; we're just going to build a two-measure one for variety.) Here, we're leaving out beat 3 (a downstroke) and the "and" of beat 4 (an upstroke) in measure 1. We're also leaving out beat 1 of measure 2 (a downstroke), and the "ands" of beats 2 and 3 (both upstrokes) in measure 2. In this strumming pattern, we're only syncopating in two places: by leaving out beat 3 of measure 1 and beat 1 of measure 2—the two places we've left out downstrokes. We've left the other upstrokes out just to create a little more character to the strum pattern. This is a good example of a real-world strum pattern, and shows that you don't have to inject too much syncopation into a strum pattern for it to work well. Too much syncopation can actually make a strum pattern lose its groovy feel.

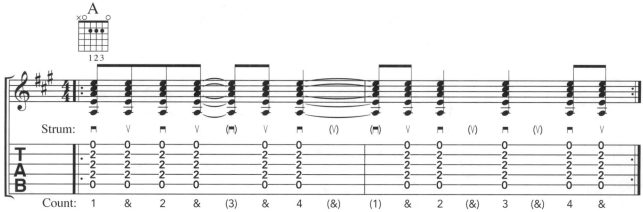

Like many syncopated strums, the last example is a pretty tricky pattern to get a handle on. Remember to play with a metronome and slow it down to where you *can* play the strum pattern. Then, gradually increase the metronome's speed until you can play it comfortably at a moderate tempo.

Now let's take this pattern and plug it into a I–IV–V chord progression. Let's also double the length of each chord to *two* measures. And, just for fun, we'll move *back* to the I chord for the last two measures:

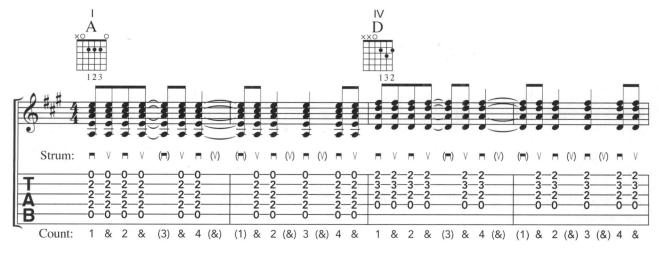

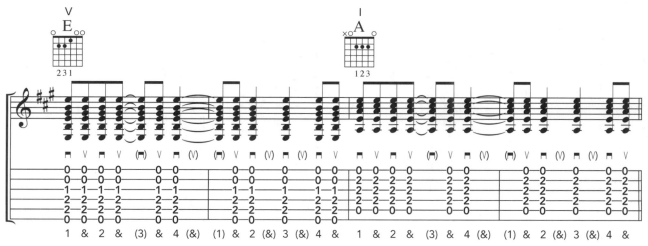

Once you hear it in a full chord progression, the previous strumming pattern starts to sound like a song. This pattern, for example, is reminiscent of songs like the Band's "Up on Cripple Creek."

I–IV–V Variations

In our last example, we switched up our I–IV–V progression by going *back* to the I chord and essentially creating a I–IV–V–I progression. The beauty of these three chords is that you can put them together in many different ways. For instance, if you go back to the *IV* chord at the end (instead of the I), you get this:

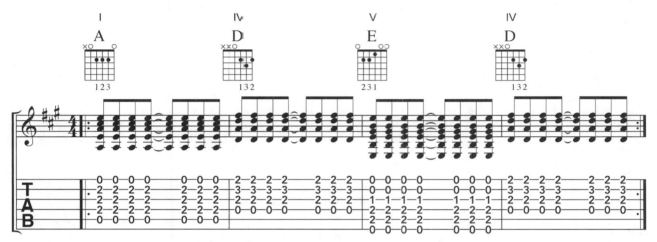

Does this sound familiar? Indeed, this I–IV–V variation is used in plenty of songs, such as "Wild Thing" by the Troggs, for instance.

Let's try another. This time, let's slip a I chord in between the IV and V chords, creating a I–IV–I–V progression.

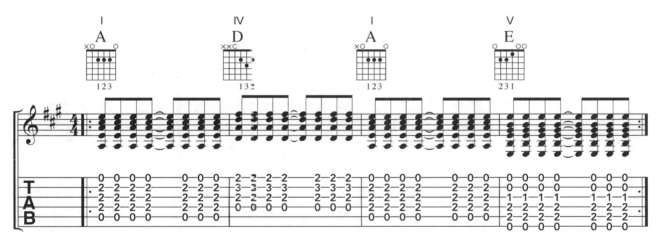

Or, you could switch the IV and V chords to get a I–V–I–IV progression:

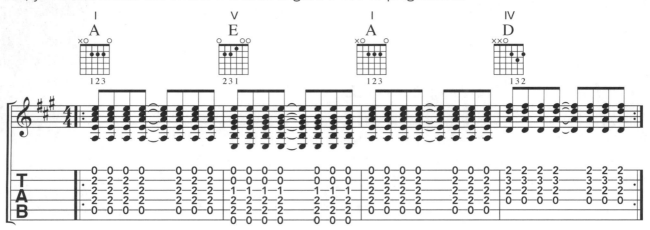

You can also string these together into longer (or shorter!) progressions. For our final example, let's build an extended progression with the I, IV, and V chords. We'll start off with our I–IV–I–V and then we'll paste a I–IV–V–I on the end for an extended eight-measure progression: I–IV–I–V–I–IV–V–I.

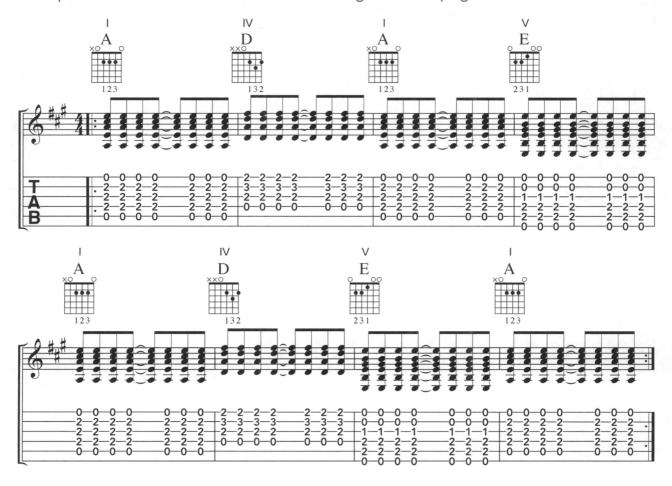

Now it's your turn. Try putting I, IV, and V chords together in different combinations to create longer (and shorter) progressions.

CHAPTER 5: MINOR CHORDS

So far, we've played only major chords. Major chords are labelled with just the letter name of the chord, and they have a "happy" sound. In this chapter, we'll learn a new chord type: the *minor* chord. Minor chords are labelled with a small "m" after the letter name and have a "sad" sound.

THE Em CHORD

To play an Em chord, place your middle and ring fingers on the second-fret space of the fifth and fourth strings, respectively. This is how the Em chord looks:

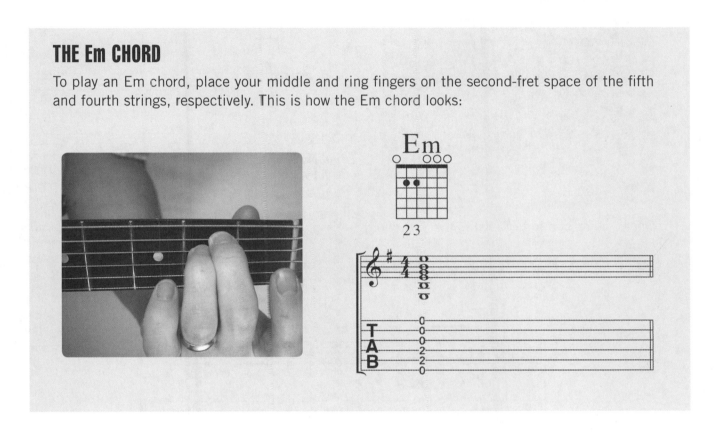

Strum through an Em chord and then switch back and forth between E (major) and Em chords to hear how they sound different. It's easy to switch between these chords, since there's only one note that's different; all you have to do is add your index finger to the third string to get an E chord:

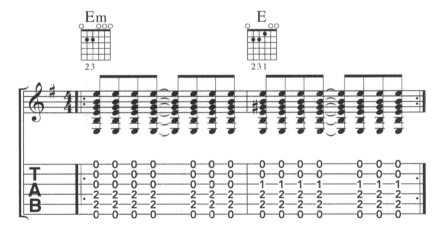

Let's learn another minor chord—the Am chord:

THE Am CHORD

To play an Am chord, place your middle and ring fingers on the second-fret space of the fourth and third strings, respectively, and place your index finger in the first-fret space of the second string. This is how the Am chord looks:

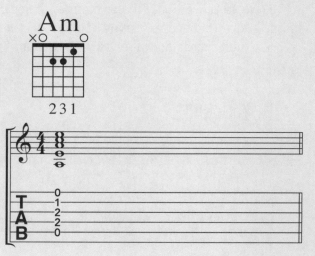

Once you're comfortable with the Am chord, let's practice switching between the Em and Am chords:

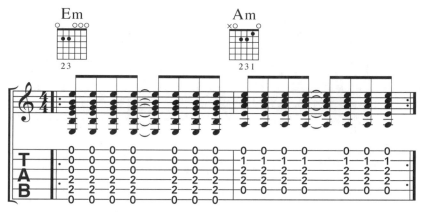

Minor and Major Chords Together

Many songs use *both* minor and major chords in their chord progressions. Let's get comfortable moving between some of our major chords and the minor chords we just learned. We'll start by using our Am chord with G, C, and D chords, sandwiching it between the G and C chords:

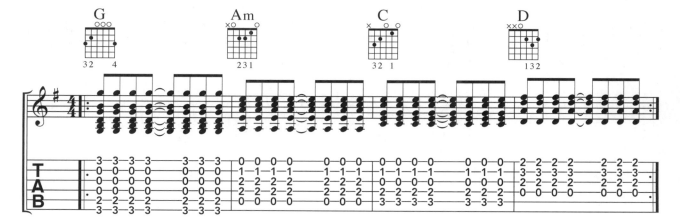

Or we could start with C, move through Am, and park on G for two measures. Let's also try out a new syncopated strumming pattern. This is basically the same pattern we've been playing, but instead of starting with a pair of eighth notes, we'll kick each measure off with a quarter note (look at the counting and strum markings if you have trouble):

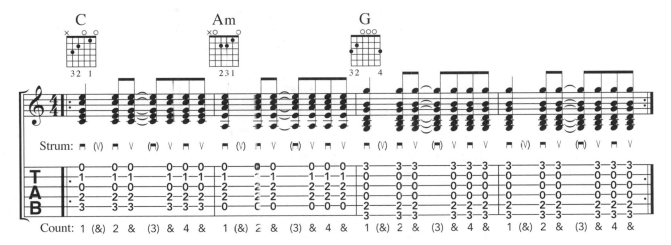

Now, let's add an Em chord in. Let's put it in our last example by replacing the G chord in the third measure with our Em chord:

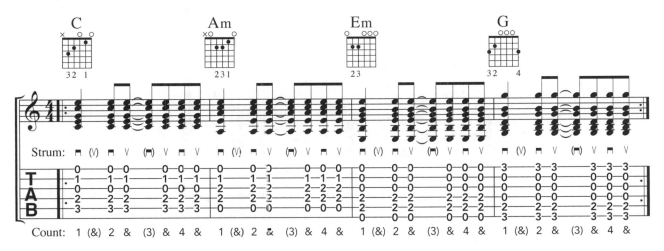

Let's try one more, just to make sure we've got these two new chords under our fingers. This one starts with Em, goes to D, then C, and ends on Am.

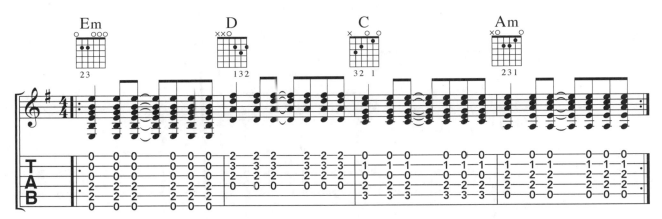

Quicker Chord Changes

We've played quite a few chord progressions up to this point, but we've always held onto each chord for at least a full measure. Sometimes, songs have chord progressions that change more quickly than that, and it's time we try this out. Let's start by switching between the Em and Am chords every *half* measure. We'll use a strum pattern built from a quarter note followed by two eighth notes to practice this chord change:

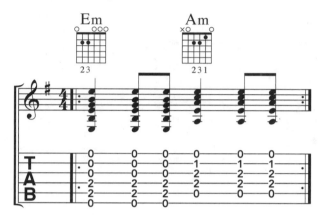

Let's try another. This time we'll play the Em–D–C–Am progression we played in the last section, but here we'll switch chords every half measure:

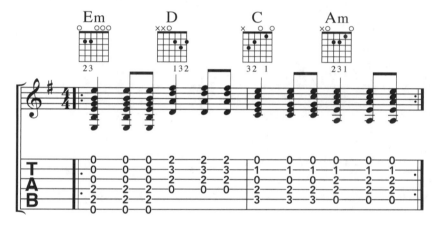

Try this out yourself on some of the chord progressions you've learned. Here's one more to keep you going: the C–Am–Em–G progression from the last section.

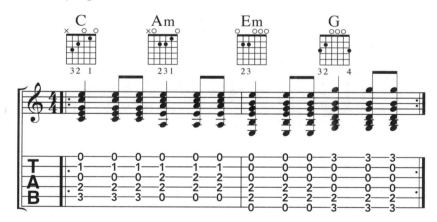

Now that you can change chords more quickly, you can vary the lengths of some of your chords. For instance, let's try our I–IV–V chord progression in the key of A (which is A–D–E, in case you need help remembering!). This time, though, let's change to the D chord midway through the first measure, and then we'll play the E chord throughout the second measure. Also check out how we're mixing our strumming up a little bit more. Here, we start with the same pattern we've been using for the quick-change chords (quarter note followed by two eighths), but we shift over to one of our syncopated patterns in the second measure.

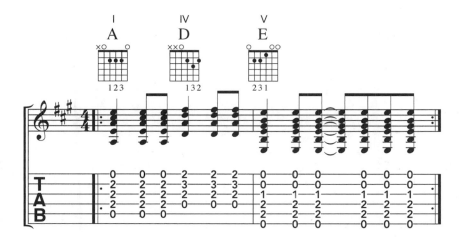

This last pattern simply speeds up the chord progression from the way we originally played it, but when we change the chords at this speed, it sounds even more like "Twist and Shout" and other classic songs.

Let's see how this affects our song "Shake It Up, Now" from several chapters ago. We'll apply this quick chord-change pattern without the syncopated strum (don't worry; we'll play this song later with syncopation!). Notice how the song goes by much quicker, but now it sounds a lot more like those other classic tunes:

SHAKE IT UP, NOW

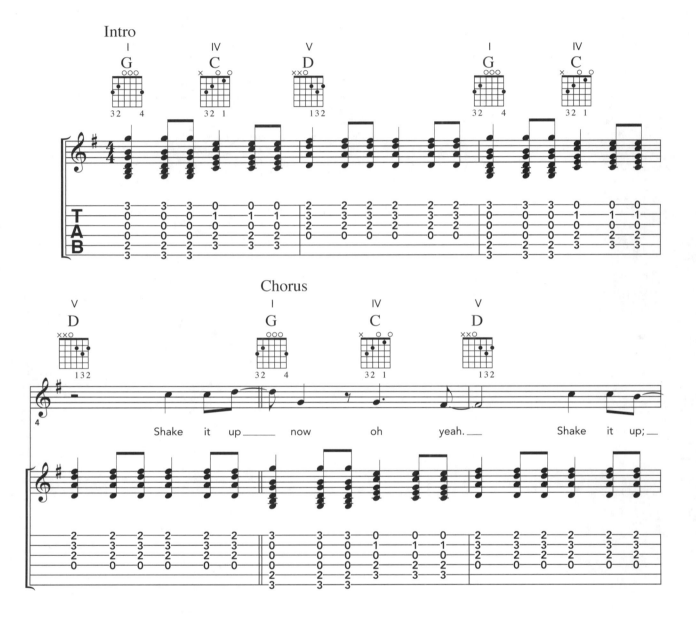

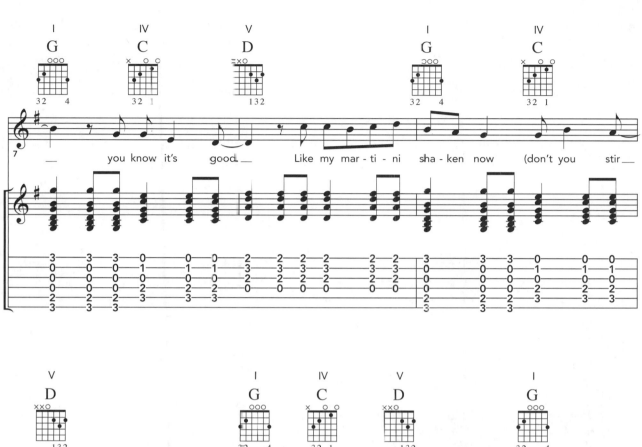

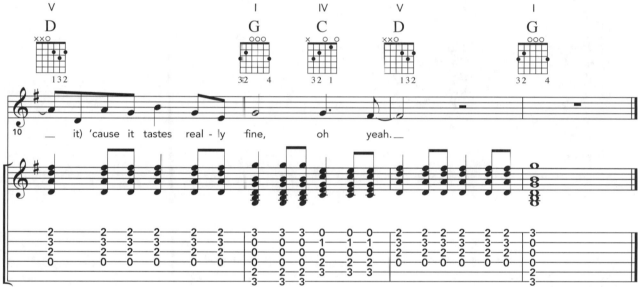

CHAPTER 6: THE ii–V–I PROGRESSION

The ii–V–I progression is popular throughout pop and rock, and it's also a staple in jazz tunes. In this lesson, we'll learn about ii–V–I progressions, but before we get to that, let's add another chord to our toolbox first:

THE Dm CHORD

To play a Dm chord, place your middle finger on the second-fret space of the third string and your ring finger on the third-fret space of the second string. Then reach up with your index finger to place it on the first-fret space of the first string. This is how a Dm chord looks:

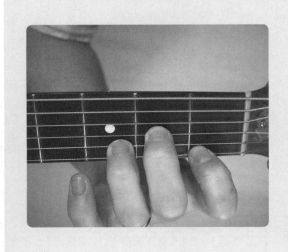
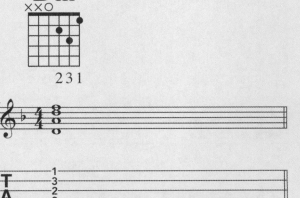

Like the D (major) chord, we only play the top four strings of the Dm chord (the four closest to the floor). Once again, when you're comfortable playing the Dm chord, practice switching between Dm and other chords. Here, we'll practice switching between Dm and Am. Then, let's practice switching between C and Dm.

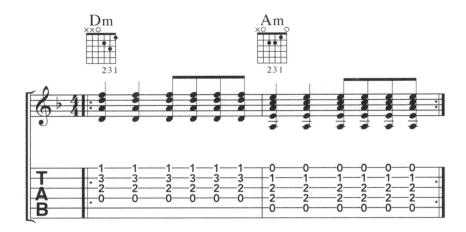

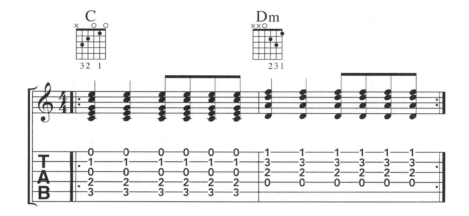

Now practice switching between the Dm chord and other chords you've already learned before moving on.

Your First ii–V–I Progression

You already know what the I and V chords are—the chords found on the first and fifth degree of whatever key you're in. So where does the ii chord come in? If you guessed it's the chord on the second degree, you're right! But one big difference is that the ii chord is minor. So, if we're in the key of D, for instance, the I chord is D, and the ii chord would be a minor chord one degree up from D. Counting up, we get: D (1), E (2). We already know that the V chord is A because we played a I–IV–V in the key of D back in Chapter 4, so that means our ii–V–I in the key of D major is Em–A–D. Let's try our ii–V–I progression out, changing chords every measure:

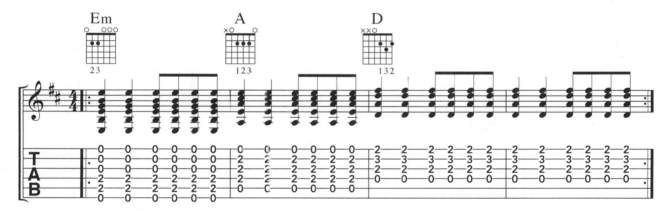

TIP: WHY IS THE "ii" A LOWERCASE "ii" IN THE ii–V–I PROGRESSION?

When we figured out our ii–V–I in the key of D, we learned that our ii chord was a minor chord. This holds the answer to our question; uppercase Roman numerals indicate major chords in a progression, and lowercase numerals indicate minor chords.

When you encounter ii–V–I progressions in songs, they can be exactly the way we just played them, but they're also often played over a two-measure span, where the ii and V chords each get two beats and the I chord gets a full measure, like this:

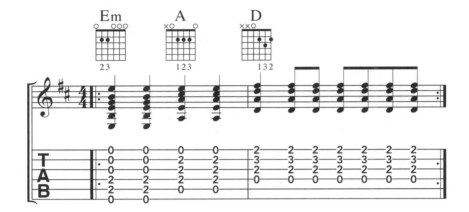

Now let's try out our ii–V–I in a song. "Saving My Kisses" strings together a series of ii–V–I progressions in the key of D, similar to a Beatles song like "All My Loving."

TIP: THE PICKUP MEASURE

Did you notice how the first measure in "Saving My Kisses" isn't complete? There are only two quarter notes! This is called a pickup measure, and many songs have them. A pickup measure is a few notes that lead into the beginning of a song, and they happen before the downbeat of the first measure. Since this pickup starts on beat 3, simply count in "1, 2" and come in on beat 3 (as shown underneath the music).

SAVING MY KISSES

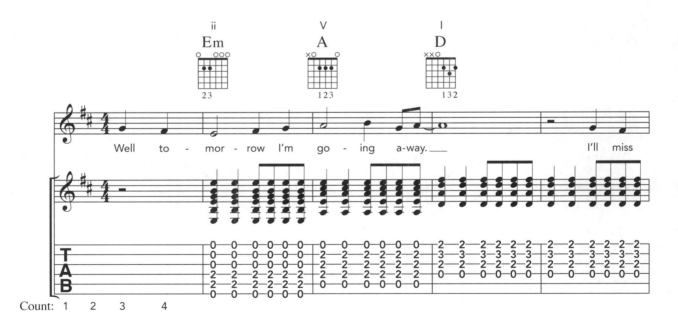

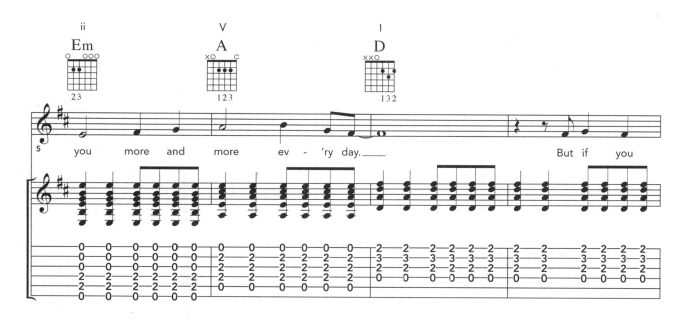

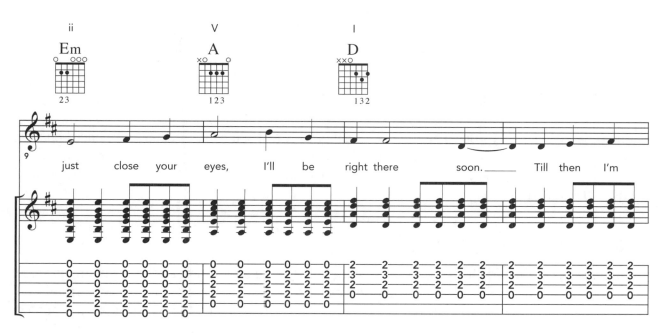

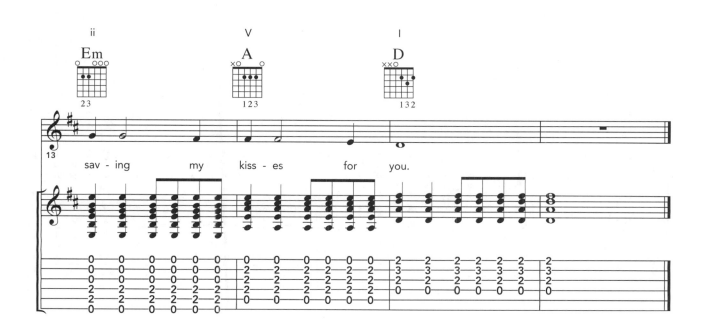

Syncopated Chord Changes

We've already learned about syncopation and how to add that into our strumming patterns. You can also syncopate your *chord changes*—a trick that can add momentum to your chord progressions, or give them a funkier sound. When you syncopate the chord change, that means you'll play a new chord on the offbeat (between beats). For instance, let's play a D–A chord change, but we'll switch to the A chord on the final upstroke of the first measure—an eighth note early—and skip the downstroke to start measure 2.

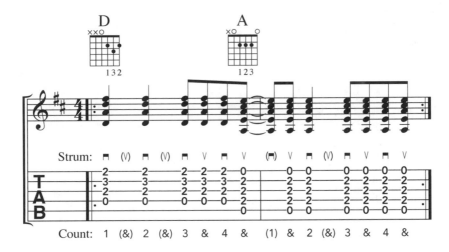

Remember to slow things down and play with a metronome if you need to. This funky chord-change work can be tricky to get under your fingers! Make sure to count along and pay attention to the strumming directions shown between the music notation and tablature (your hand will be moving constantly up and down).

TIP: CHORD CHANGE TRICK, REVISITED

Remember that you can change your chord a little early, and strum through the open strings while you're doing that. The open-stringed strum goes by so quickly that it's hardly noticeable, and guitarists of all levels do this all the time. This trick really helps out when you play syncopated chord changes, because you need time to get your hands in place for that syncopated chord.

Let's try this out with a ii–V–I progression. Here, the syncopated chord change happens at the end of the first measure, when changing from the Em to the A chord:

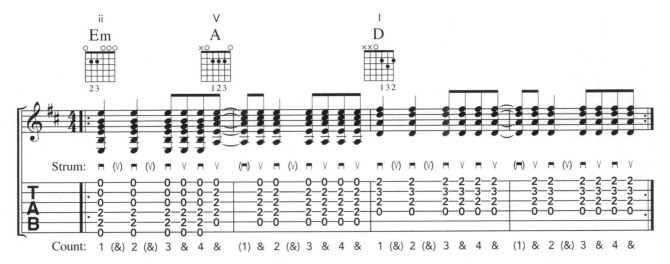

TIP: BITE-SIZE STRUM PATTERNS

Notice how, in the previous example, the strum pattern is exactly the same in measures 3–4 as it is in measures 1–2. While you can certainly have longer strum patterns, repeating one- or two-measure patterns is often the best way to back up a song; much longer strum patterns can distract the listener from the song itself (and really long patterns can start to sound like no pattern at all!)

Also notice how the strum pattern and chord progression interact with each other. Since we change chords more quickly in the first two measures, we have a syncopated chord change. In measures 3–4, we still have syncopation in the same place, but we just don't have a chord change there. The varied chord-change length creates a little interest, while the repeated strum pattern keeps things sounding grounded and consistent.

Now let's try a syncopated chord change with a quicker ii–V–I progression—one that lasts only two measures:

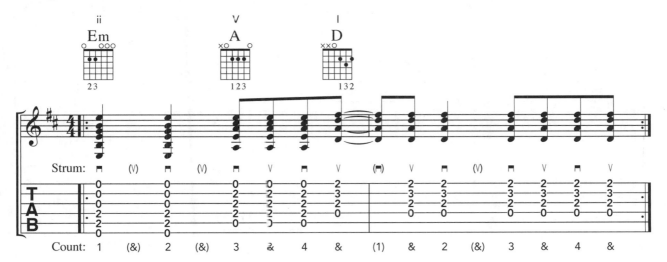

Let's try another syncopated chord change. Here, we'll take our tried-and-true I–IV–V in the key of A (A–D–E) and syncopate the E chord change the same way we did in the previous example—we'll change on the last upstroke of measure 1, again skipping the downbeat on measure 2. But we'll *also* syncopate the strum right before the chord change by leaving out the downstroke on beat 4. Make sure to count along (and slow things down if you need to!).

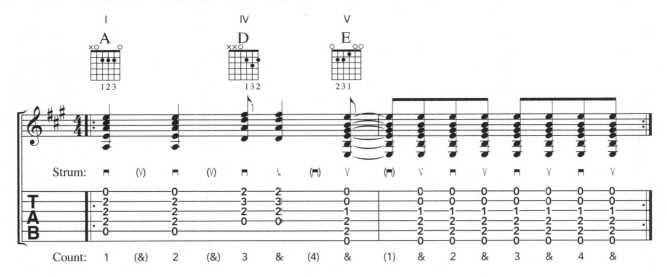

As you can see, this gives the I–IV–V even more of that "Twist and Shout"-type character. So piecing together a little syncopation with varied chord-change length can really spice up our strum patterns and songs!

Let's finish this chapter by playing "Shake It Up, Now" (from earlier in the book), but this time we'll use the syncopated strum and chord change from the previous example to make it sound even more like the classic hits.

SHAKE IT UP, NOW

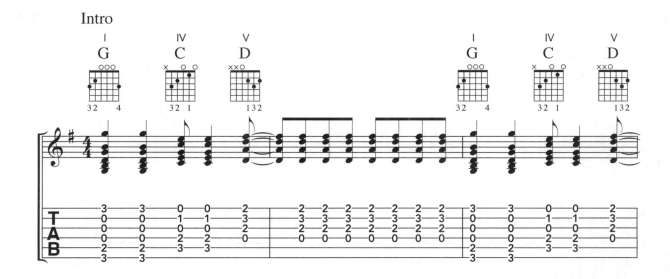

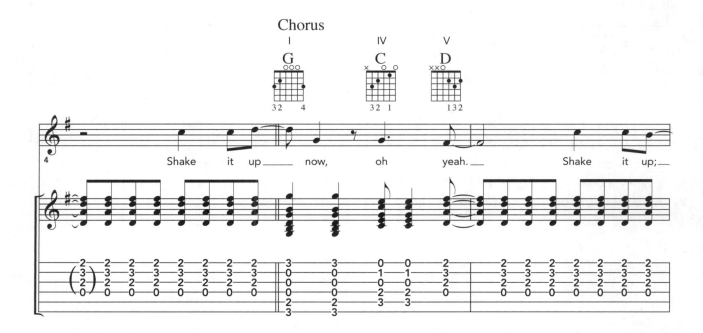

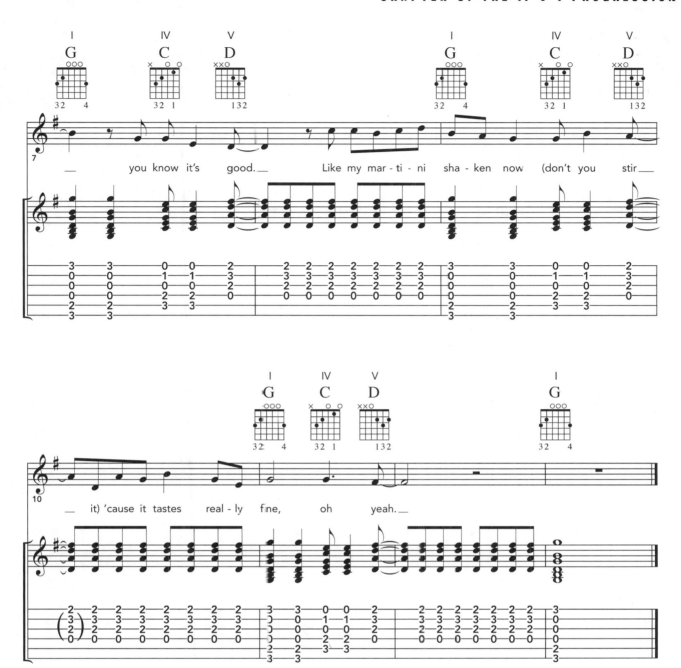

CHAPTER 7: BASS-NOTE STRUM PATTERNS

Strumming is a great way to play songs, but sometimes you need something a little different, and playing bass-note strum patterns is a good way to mix things up. A *bass-note strum* pattern sounds exactly as you'd expect. Start by playing the bass note of a chord, then follow that up with some strums. Let's try this out with an E chord using quarter notes:

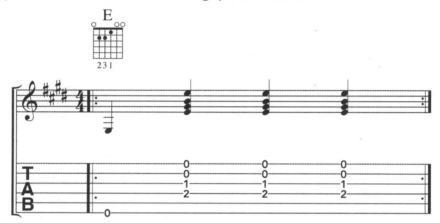

Picking only one string may feel awkward at first, since we've only been strumming chords so far. So slow your tempo down, if you need to, until you're comfortable picking the bass note and following it up with strums (of course, use a metronome as well, if you have one!).

Next, let's speed our strumming up to eighth notes, but we'll leave that bass note as a quarter note:

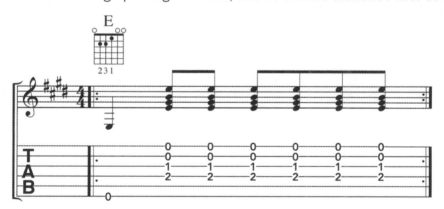

This is a fairly standard bass-note strum pattern found on many songs, and you can use this pattern for any six-string chord, since the bass note for that chord will be on the lowest (sixth) string. Let's try it with a G chord:

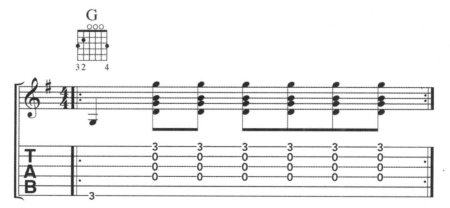

Of course, if your chord is a five-string chord, you'll need to pluck the bass note on the *fifth* string. Let's try this out with a C chord:

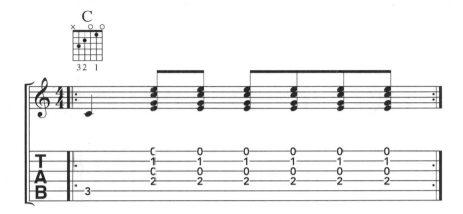

Any five-string chords will use this pattern, such as A or Am. Let's try it out with Am, just to make sure we have the pattern down:

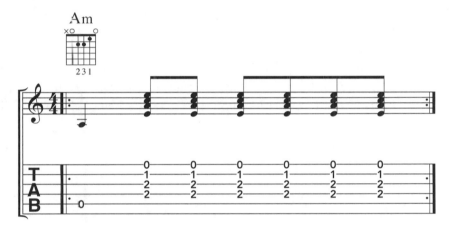

Finally, we'll have to adapt the pattern again for any four-string chords we play. As you'd expect, we'll play the bass note on the fourth string for these chords. Let's try this out with a D chord:

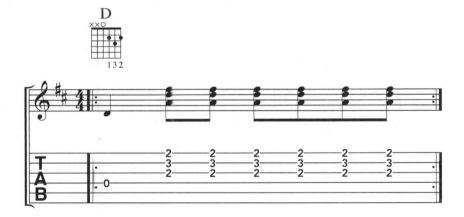

Now that we have the bass-note strum pattern down, let's try it out with a full chord progression—a ii–V–I in D, which is Em–A–D (we played this in the previous chapter).

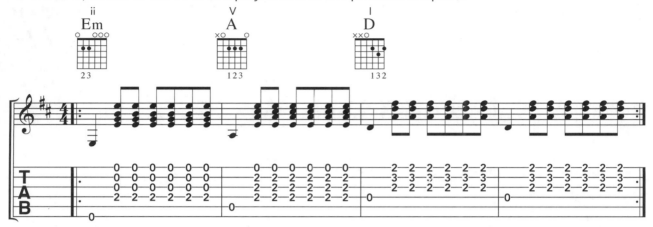

The ii–V–I Progression in G

Now let's transfer our ii–V–I progression to another key. To play it in the key of G, all we have to do is figure out what the ii, V, and I chords would be. As we've already learned, the I chord is the same letter as the key we're in, so our I chord will be G. Then, we'll simply count up the G scale to find the other two chords. The ii chord's built from the second degree, so we'll count up: G (1), A (2). So the ii chord is Am. (Remember that our ii chord, and any lowercase Roman numeral chord, is minor.) For the V chord, we'll count up to the fifth degree of the scale. Counting up, we get D as the V chord: G (1), A (2), B (3), C (4), D (5). So our ii–V–I in the key of G is Am–D–G:

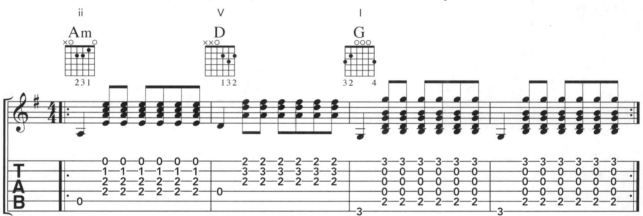

The ii–V–I Progression in C

Since we're getting better at figuring out which chords fit into these progressions, let's figure out a ii–V–I in another key: the key of C. First, we know that a C chord will be the I chord (since it's the same letter as the key we're in). Next, let's count up to the fifth degree of the C scale to see what the ii and V chords will be: C (1), D (2), E (3), F (4), G (5). So the ii chord will be a Dm chord, and the V chord will be a G chord. Let's plug those into our ii–V–I progression, and we get Dm–G–C:

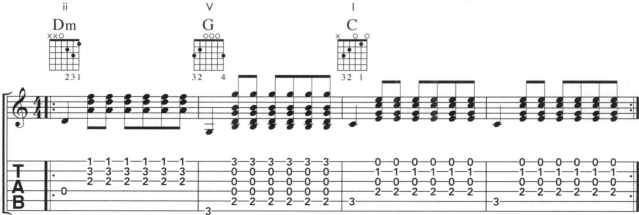

Changing Chords in the Middle of a Measure

When you're playing bass-note strum patterns, what happens when you change chords in the middle of a measure? There are several things you could do. One option is to simply strum the chord change in the middle of the measure, only playing bass notes for chords that fall on beat 1 of any measure. Let's try that out with our ii–V–I in C:

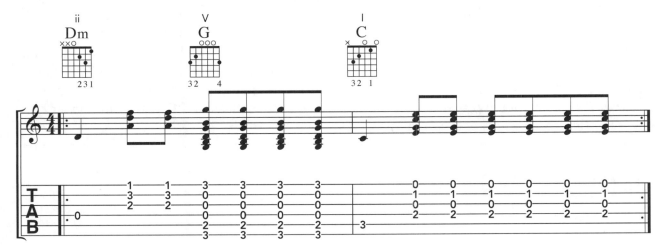

The other option is to play a bass note for that mid-measure chord change as well. Let's try this out:

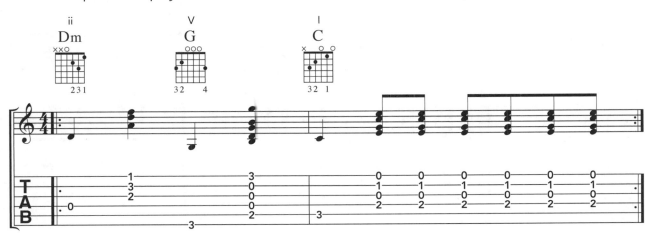

Here, I've left out some of the eighth-note strums—especially right before a quick change—to make the switch a little easier. Experiment with this yourself for any chord progression, and use the patterns you find most comfortable.

Breaking Away from "Standard" Chord Progressions

The I–IV–V and ii–V–I progressions—along with many others—are standard chord progressions commonly known to musicians. But many songs don't include those exact chords in the same order; in reality, many songs mix these chords up a bit or include those chord progressions within a larger progression. We've briefly explored this in earlier chapters, so let's finish this lesson by looking at another song that deviates from our standard chord progressions.

"Sammy Snake" uses bass-note strum patterns to create an effect similar to songs like the Beatles' "Rocky Raccoon" or the Shins' "New Slang." The song is in the key of G, and check out how the verse cycles through a quick ii–V–I over the next four measures (and repeats these eight measures to complete the verse). In the chorus, the song mixes up I, ii, IV, and V chords in other ways, creating a nice contrast to the verse section.

TIP: MULTIPLE ENDINGS

We've seen repeat signs, but this song is the first time we've seen *multiple endings*, which are shown by horizontal brackets over numbered endings (see measures 23–25). The first time you play through the chorus of the song, follow the first ending to play measures 23 and 24, and then follow the repeat sign (the double horizontal line with two dots) *back* to the beginning of the chorus (measure 17). On the second time through, skip that first ending and go directly to the second ending. This means you'll play measure 22, move directly on to measure 25, then continue on with the song (in this case, it's only several measures).

SAMMY SNAKE

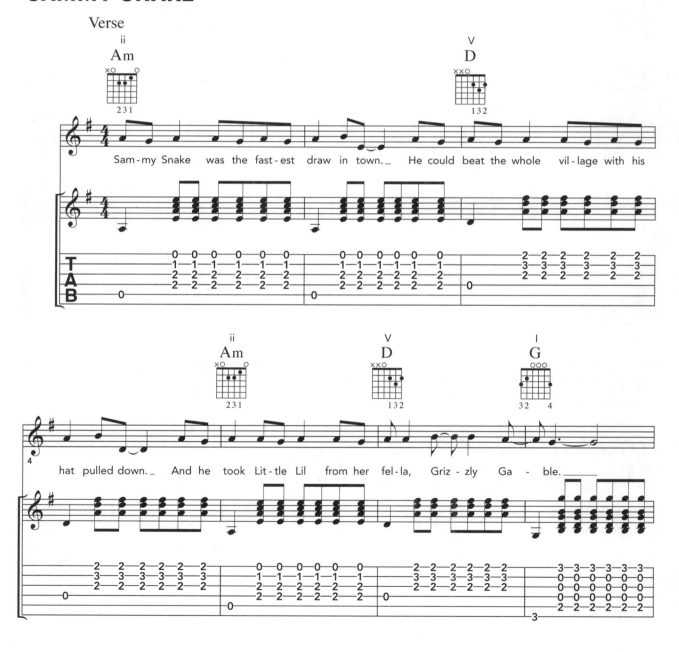

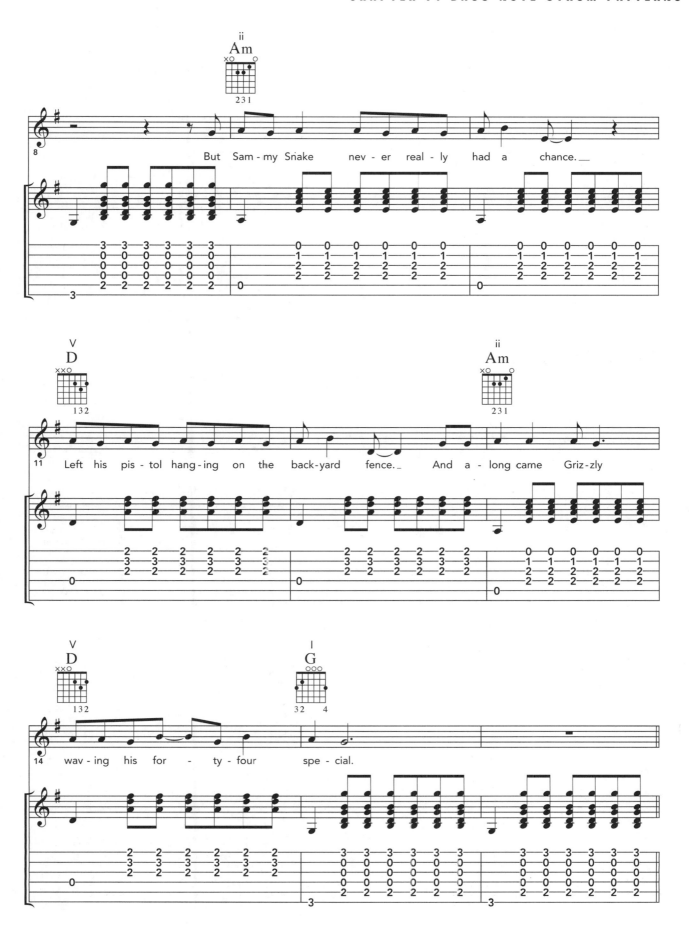

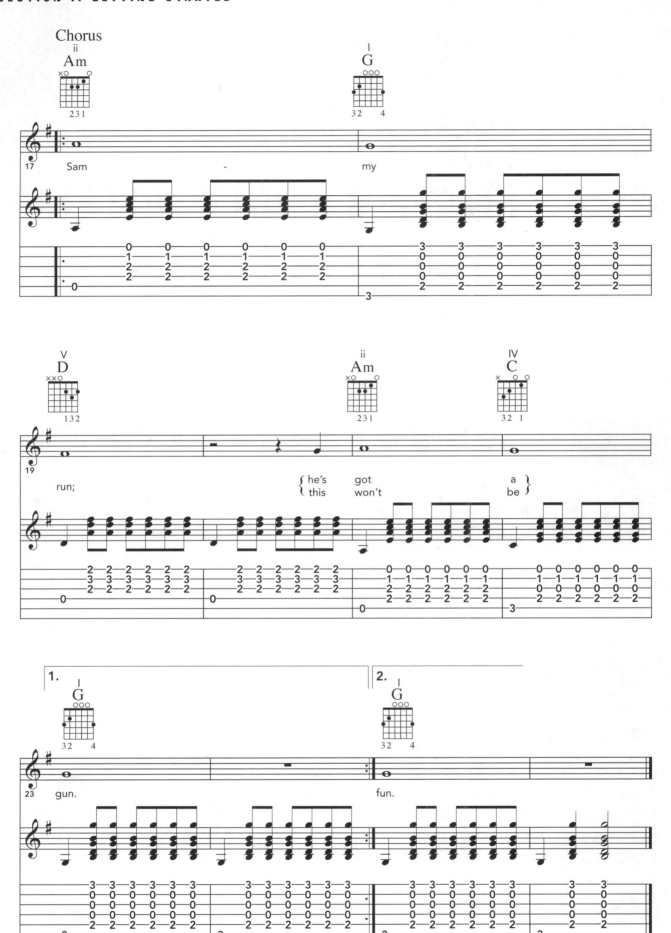

CHAPTER 8: DOMINANT SEVENTH CHORDS

Dominant seventh chords are thicker sounding chords than the major or minor chords we've worked with so far. They're a staple of pop, rock, and especially the blues. Dominant seventh chords are often simply called "seventh chords" and are labelled with a numeral "7" after the letter name.

THE E7 CHORD

An easy way to find the E7 shape is to start with an E chord, then simply remove your ring finger from the second fret of the fourth string. Here is how an E7 chord looks:

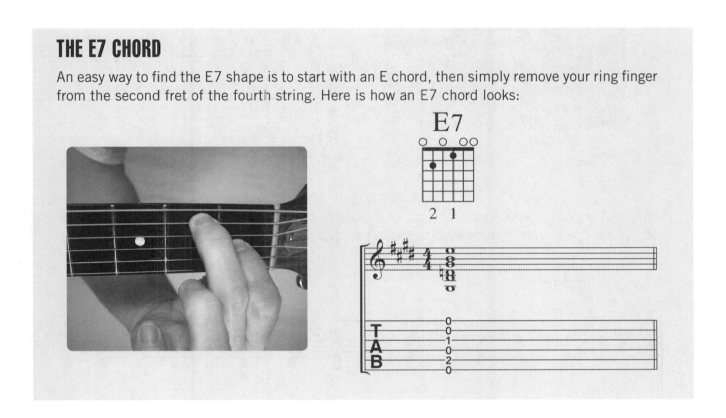

The E7 chord isn't too tricky to get a handle on since it's so similar to a standard E chord. Now let's switch between our E7 chord and an E chord so we can hear how a dominant seventh chord differs from a major chord.

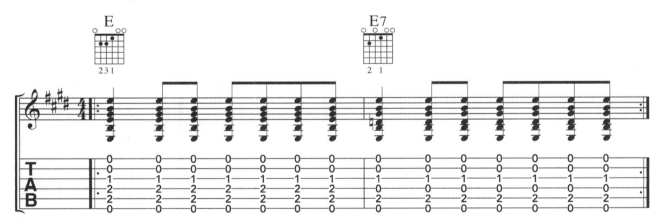

THE A7 CHORD

To play an A7 chord, place your middle and ring fingers on the second-fret space of the fourth and second strings, respectively. This is how the A7 chord looks:

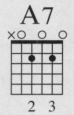

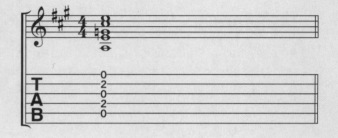

Now that we know two seventh chords, let's practice switching between them (remember, they're often called "seventh" chords instead of the full "dominant seventh" name.)

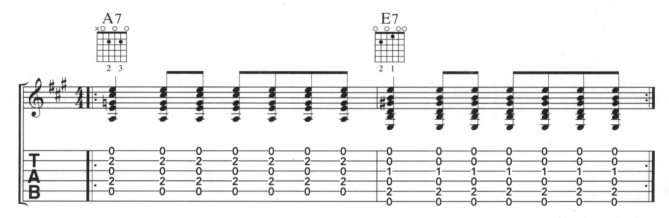

Of course, our bass-note strum patterns will work fine with these chords, as well:

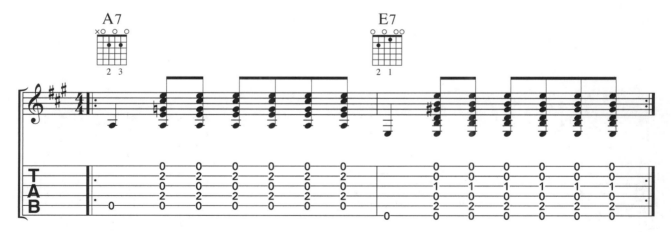

The Dominant Seventh as the V Chord

Dominant seventh chords work well in many places, especially as a V chord in a progression. For instance, it's common to rock between the I and V chords. Let's try using our A7 chord as the V in a I–V progression, which will be a D–A7 progression in the key of D (we learned the I, IV, and V chords in the key of D back in Chapter 4):

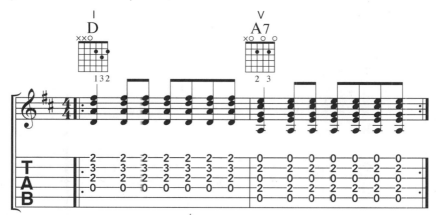

Now let's try this using our E7 chord as the V in a I–V progression. Here, our I–V progression will be A–E7 in the key of A (Again, we learned our I, IV, and V chords in the key of A back in Chapter 4.):

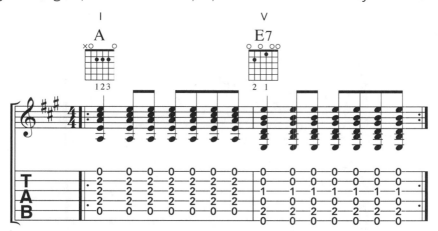

Compare the difference between a major V chord and a dominant seventh V chord; note how they resolve back to the I chord:

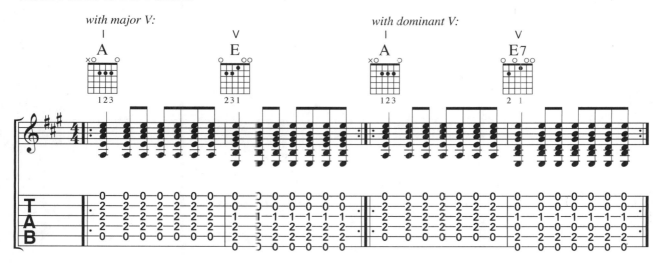

Do you hear how the dominant seventh chord pulls back to the I chord even more strongly? Because of this, it's common to use the seventh chord right before heading back to the I chord to make that chord change even stronger.

Dominant Seventh Chords in I–IV–V Progressions

Since the dominant seventh chord works great as a V chord, let's try using it in a I–IV–V progression. We'll start in the key of D. Back in Chapter 4, we learned that a I–IV–V progression in D is D–G–A, so when we substitute in our dominant seventh chord we get D–G–A7:

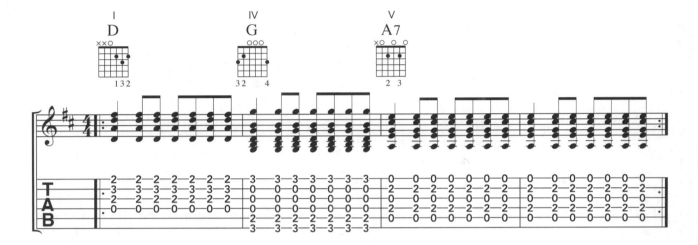

Now let's try a I–IV–V in the key of A, using a dominant seventh chord for the V. Again, back in Chapter 4, we learned that a I–IV–V in the key of A is A–D–E, so when we substitute in that dominant seventh chord for the V, we get A–D–E7:

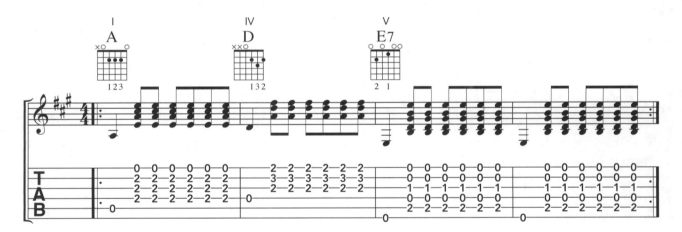

Let's try one more trick. Since that dominant chord resolves more strongly back to the I, we want it as the last chord before we repeat back to the I. But we can keep a regular major V chord (in this case E) for the measure before. This creates a little more motion because we move from the E to E7, instead of parking on either one of those chords for two measures:

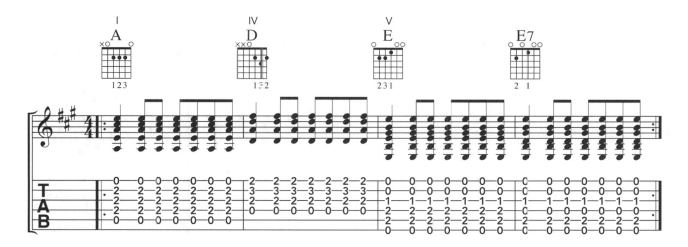

Let's try this out with "Shake It Up, Now" to see how one small enhancement can help give our tune even more of that vintage sound. Before we do, though, we need to learn one more new seventh chord: D7. (Remember that this song is in the key of G, so our I–IV–V is now G–C–D7.)

THE D7 CHORD

To play a D7 chord, place your middle and ring fingers on the second-fret space of the third and first strings, respectively, and then place your index finger in the first-fret space of the second string. This is how the D7 chord looks:

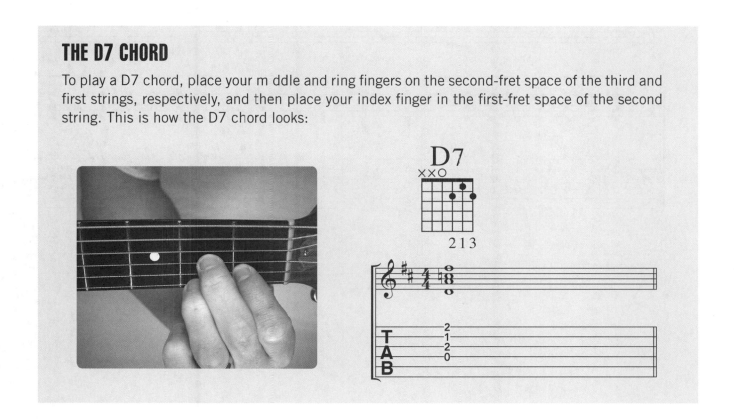

SHAKE IT UP, NOW

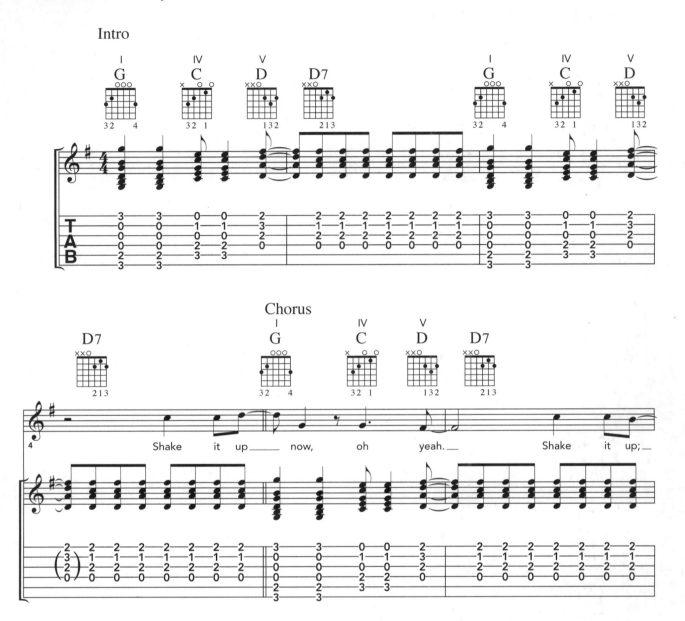

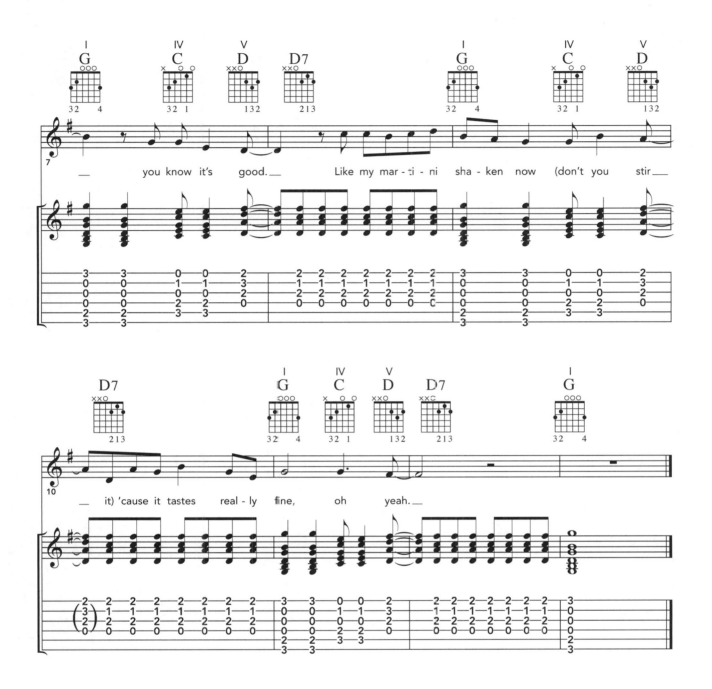

SECTION II:
Moving On

CHAPTER 9: ALTERNATE-BASS STRUMMING

Alternate-bass strumming takes our bass-note strum patterns a step further by alternating between different bass notes. To see how this works, let's start with a bass-note strum pattern on a D chord:

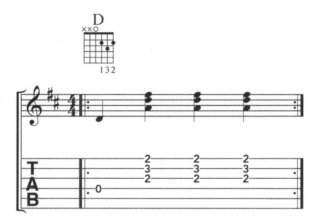

Next, we'll play that bass note twice in a measure—on beats 1 and 3:

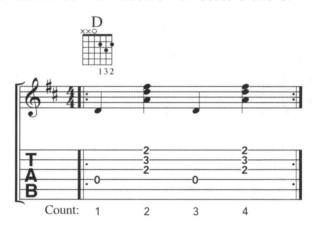

Now it's time for the alternate bass. Instead of playing a D bass note on beat 3, we'll move down to the open A string to play this note, but we'll keep our D bass note on beat 1:

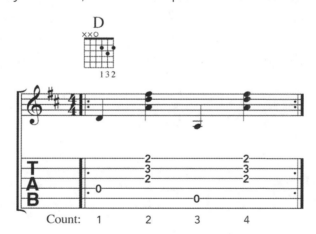

This is a little trickier than always playing the same bass note, so give yourself some time to get comfortable with it. The bonus is that this gives a little more motion to our strum patterns because the bass note is moving around.

You also often have several options about which bass notes to alternate with. On our D chord, for instance, we could instead play our *third* string on beat 3, which gives a higher bass sound:

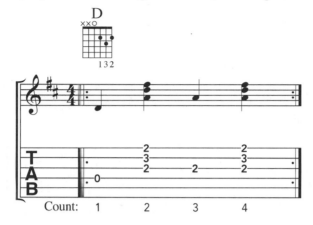

Let's try this out with an E chord now. Since our bass note on the E chord is the lowest string, we can't go any lower on beat 3, so we'll alternate that low sixth-string bass note with the note on the fifth string, which we'll play on beat 3:

It's also common to alternate bass notes on an E chord between the sixth and *fourth* strings, like this:

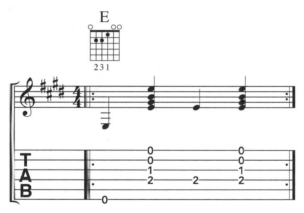

This might take a little getting used to, since you're skipping a string on your bass note, but it's another nice sound that's worth the work. In fact, this sixth/fourth string bass note pattern is the most common one used for a G chord:

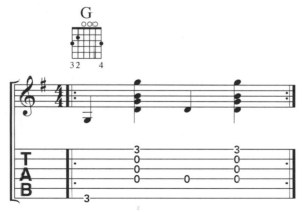

You *can* alternate between the sixth and fifth strings for a G chord, as well, though. Here's how that sounds:

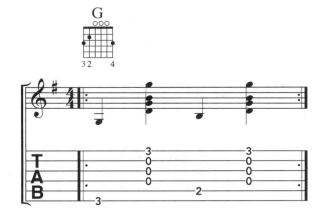

Now let's try alternate-bass strumming with an A chord, which has its bass note on the fifth string. Here, we can alternate our bass note between the fifth and sixth string, like this:

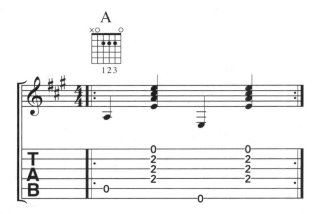

But we can also alternate our bass note between the fifth and fourth strings for our A chord, as well:

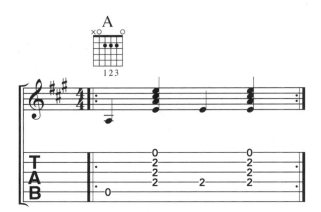

For our D7 chord, we can play the same alternate-bass strum patterns as we do with a standard D chord. We can either alternate between the fourth and fifth strings, as shown in the first example below, or we can alternate between the fourth and third strings, as shown in the second example below:

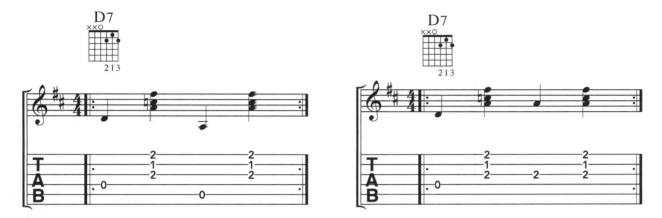

Fretting New Bass Notes

Some chords require you to rock your fretting fingers between two notes so that you can play alternate-bass strumming. Let's try a C chord. If we alternate between the fifth and fourth strings for our bass notes, it sounds just fine:

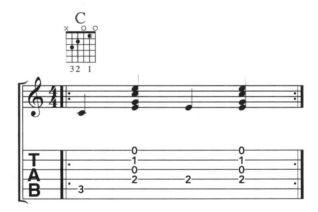

But when we try and rock between the fifth and sixth strings, that low bass note sounds a little too muddy:

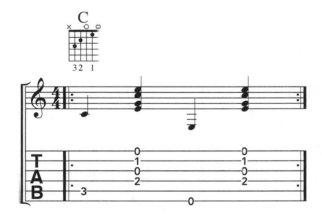

So we'll get around this problem by fretting the sixth string at the third fret. You can do this one of two ways. The less common way to do this is to use your pinky on the third fret of the fifth string and move your ring finger down to the third fret of the sixth string, like this:

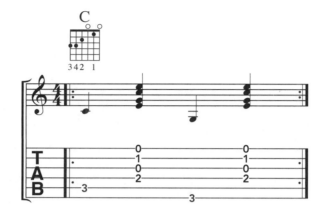

But you can also give that ring finger double duty, rocking it between the fifth and sixth strings to play each bass note as it comes along. This is the more common way to play alternate-bass strumming with a C chord; it takes a bit of work to get comfortable with it, but provides a nice flowing sound when you've mastered it:

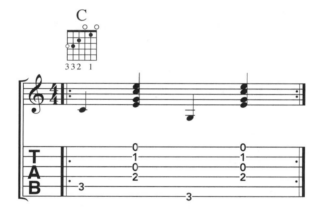

Of all these ways to play the C chord, choose the way you like best for any song or chord progression.

Let's learn one more chord before we move on: the C7 chord.

THE C7 CHORD

To play a C7 chord, start with a C chord and then place your pinky on the third-fret space of the third string. This is how the C7 chord looks:

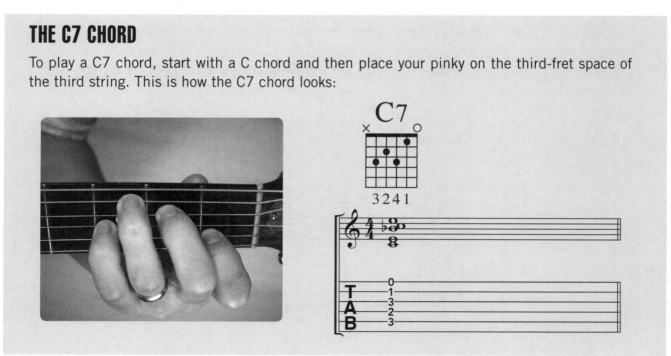

We can easily play alternate-bass strumming with our C7 chord by alternating between our fourth and third strings for the bass notes, as we just did with the C chord:

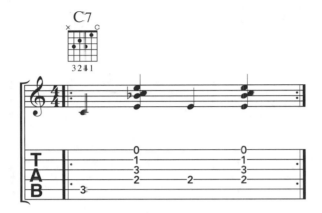

But what about when we want a *lower* bass note? For our new C7 chord, we can't fret that low sixth-string bass note with another finger, since all of our fingers are used to fret the chord! So, we'll have to rock between the fifth and sixth string, like we just did with the C chord:

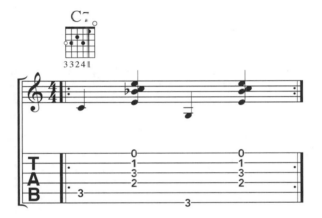

Dominant Seventh Chords in ii–V–I Progressions

In the last chapter, we used dominant seventh chords in I–IV–V and I–V progressions, but we can also use them in plenty of other progressions. Now let's try them out in ii–V–I progressions. Let's start by using our D7 chord as the V chord in a ii–V–I. Back in Chapter 7 (Bass-Note Strum Patterns), we learned that a ii–V–I in the key of G is Am–D–G. We'll just substitute in our D7 chord for the D chord to get Am–D7–G. We'll practice our alternate-bass strumming as well:

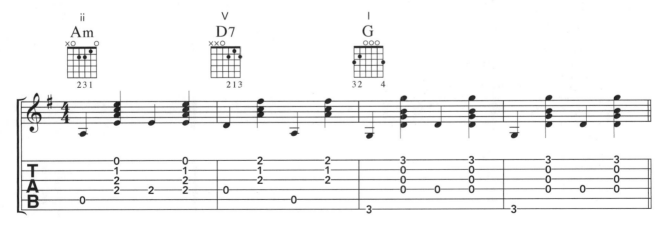

Let's try this out with one more ii–V–I progression by using an A7 as the V chord. In Chapter 6, we learned that a ii–V–I in the key of D is Em–A–D, so we'll substitute our A7 chord in for the A chord to get Em–A7–D. We'll try one more new thing in this example. Let's play eighth-note strums after each quarter-note bass note. Remember to slow things down if you need to!

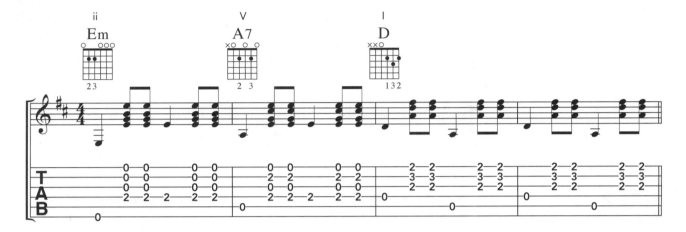

Let's finish this lesson by taking our alternate-bass strumming for a spin in a song. We'll use the strum pattern from the previous example and put it into "Saving My Kisses" (from Chapter 6). Aside from the alternate-bass strumming pattern, let's also use the dominant seventh A chord as the V chord, instead of a major A chord:

SAVING MY KISSES

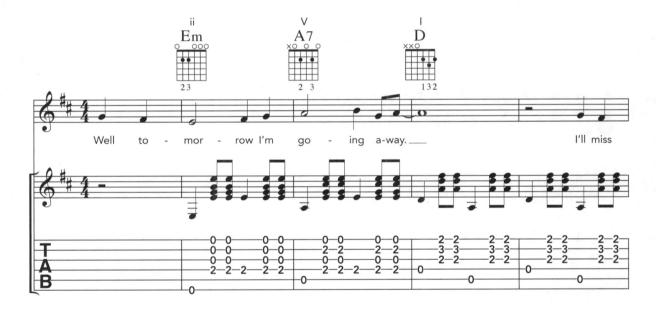

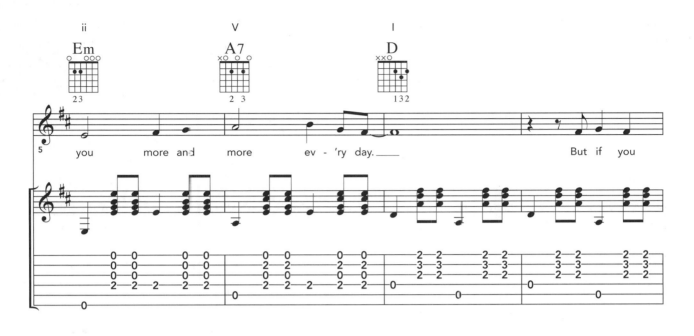

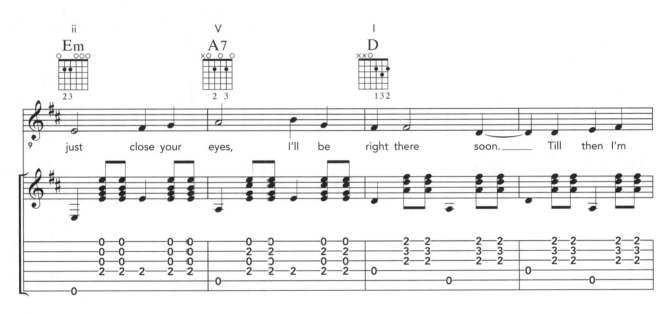

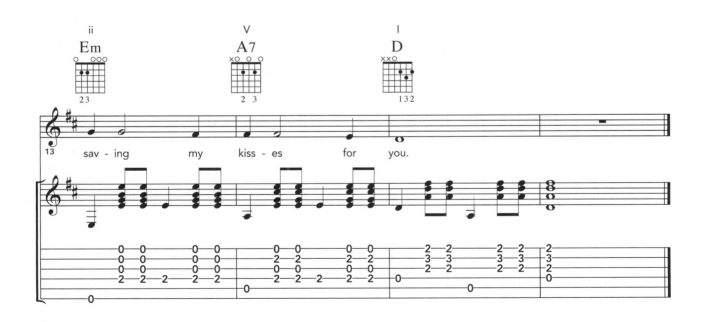

CHAPTER 10: THE MINOR i–iv–v PROGRESSION

So far, we've played I–IV–V progressions in major keys, but we can also play them in minor keys, too. Since minor chords use lowercase Roman numerals, a similar minor progression would be labelled i–iv–v.

Let's try out a minor i–iv–v in the key of Am. We know that a I–IV–V in the key of A is A–D–E, and we can simply substitute minor chords in to make our minor i–iv–v (which will be Am–Dm–Em):

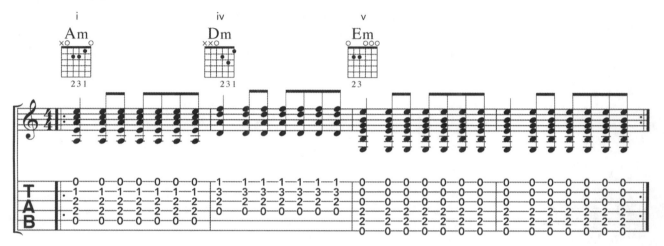

Now let's try our i–iv–v progression using alternate-bass strumming:

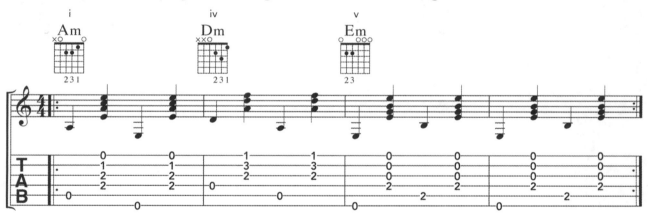

Let's explore how we can change our sound by varying our bass notes. In the previous example, we alternated between lower bass notes for our Am and Dm chords. Now let's see how this sounds when we alternate between higher notes for these chords:

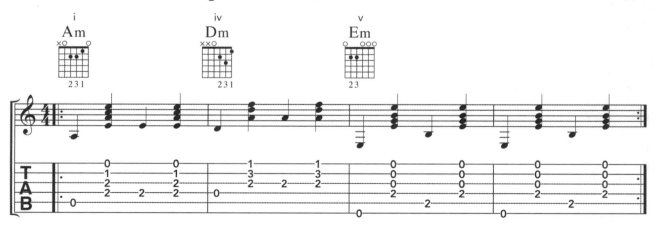

This sounds a little lighter or "brighter," and we can brighten it up even more by alternating our bass note between the sixth and fourth strings for the Em chord (instead of the sixth and fifth strings).

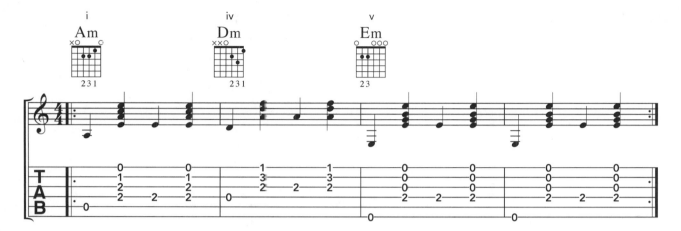

There are many ways to play these alternate-bass patterns. For instance, let's take the previous example, but now alternate between the fourth and fifth strings for the Dm bass notes. This creates a nice balance, as the Am and Em chords are moving up for their bass notes, while the Dm chord is sandwiched between those two chords and moving down.

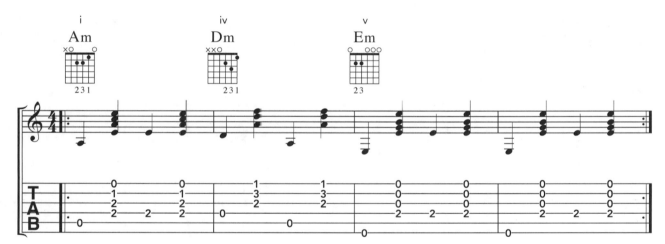

Major or Dominant V in Minor Progressions

In minor keys, it's common to substitute a major or dominant seventh V chord for the minor v chord, because they resolve more strongly back to the i chord (especially the dominant seventh chord). Let's compare the three by plugging them into a i–v progression:

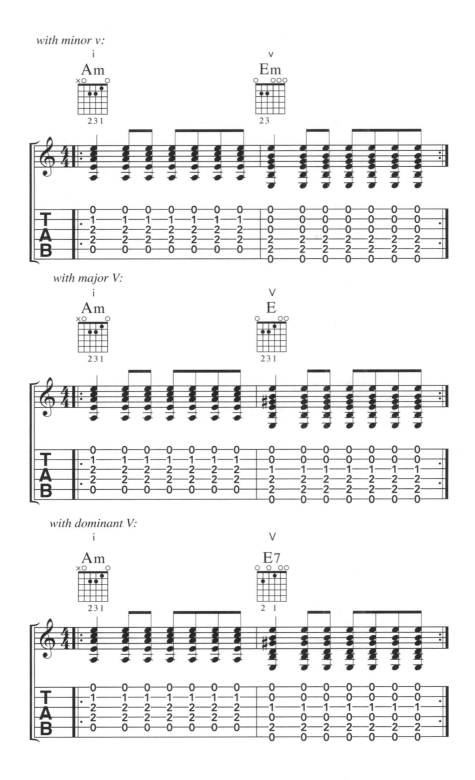

Let's hear how these sound in the context of a chord progression. Here's our i–iv–V with a major V chord. We'll play it with an alternate-bass strumming pattern:

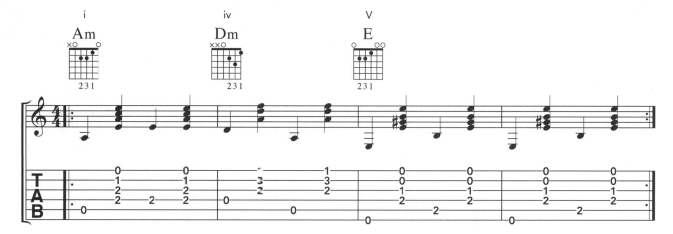

Now let's try the same thing with our dominant seventh chord as the V:

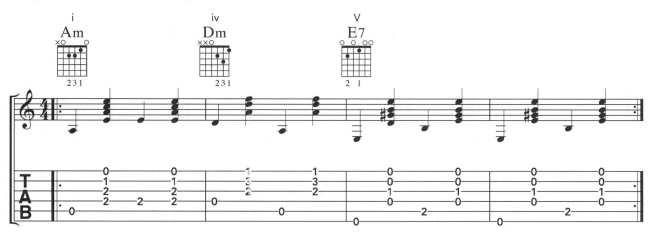

Let's try it one more time. This time, we'll move from the major chord in the third measure to the dominant seventh chord in the fourth measure—something we explored at the end of Chapter 8. We'll also alternate our bass note between the sixth and fourth strings for the E and E7 chords to really bring out the motion from the E to the E7 chord (that's the string that has a different note in it between the two chords, so listen to how this highlights that note).

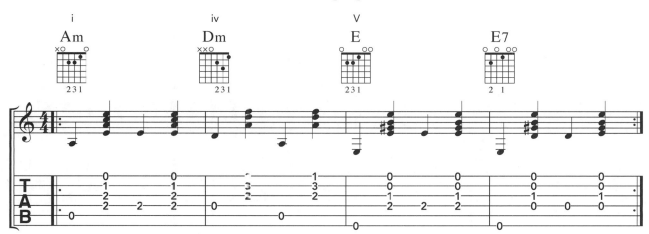

CHAPTER 11: THE BLUES PROGRESSION

The 12-bar blues is one of the most popular progressions to play. It only takes three chords—the I, IV, and V chords—to play the blues, so you're already equipped to play the blues in quite a few different keys. The only tricky thing about the progression is that it's long—12 measures long! But once you learn how it goes, you'll never forget its unique chord structure. Let's start out by looking at the most basic 12-bar blues progression in the key of A.

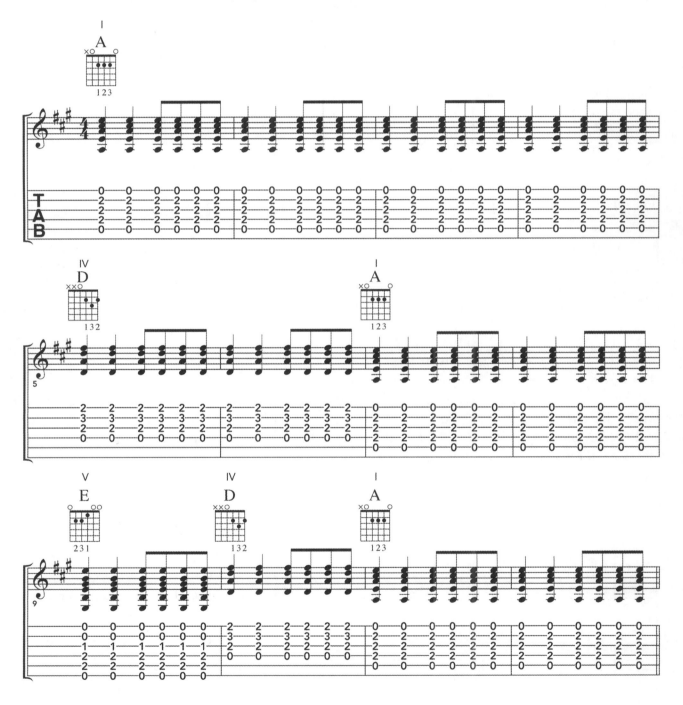

As you can see, the progression moves as follows:

- the I chord (A) for four measures
- the IV chord (D) for two measures
- back to the I chord (A) for two more measures
- the V chord (E) for just one measure
- down through the IV chord again (D) for one measure
- and ends on the I chord (A) for two measures.

So a map of the chords would look like this:

You may also see chord progressions written out like the following example, with just a notation staff and slashes. This helps you visualize the whole progression without strum patterns and tablature turning the example into multiple pages, making it hard to see the overall progression. When you see something like this, you get to play whatever strumming pattern you want to. For the rest of this chapter, we'll write out our examples this way, with chords over slashes in notation. To keep things from getting too confusing, I'll play the same strum pattern from the first example throughout the lesson, but you can feel free to vary your strum patterns as you like.

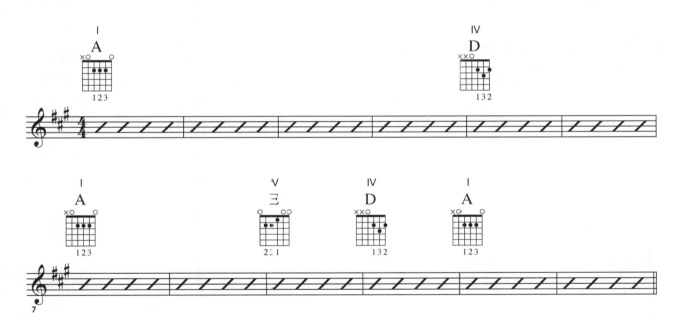

It's very common to use dominant seventh chords for *all three* chords in a blues progression. Let's try this out with our 12-bar blues in A:

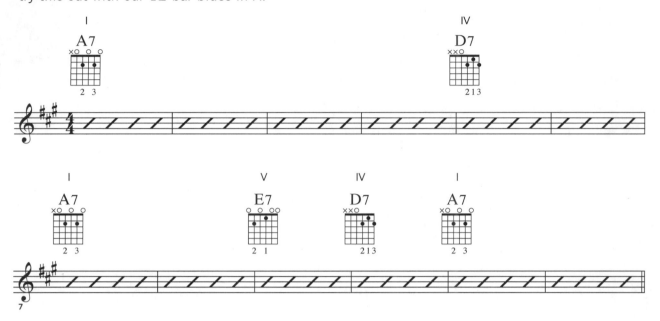

TIP: EITHER DOMINANT SEVENTH OR MAJOR WILL DRIVE THE BLUES

Dominant seventh chords are the most common way to play the blues, and we'll use dominant seventh chords throughout the rest of this chapter for our 12-bar blues progressions. But major chords are used in the blues, too, and will work fine in place of these seventh chords. Practice them both ways, and feel free to interchange the two as you experiment with the blues on your own.

The Turnaround

Most 12-bar blues progressions aren't played exactly like the ones we just played, and that's because many blues progressions include a *turnaround* at the end of the form. A "turnaround" is literally used to "turn around" the form and head it back to the beginning. Since the V chord is so good at resolving back to the I chord, the turnaround is often just the V chord plugged in for the last measure, like this:

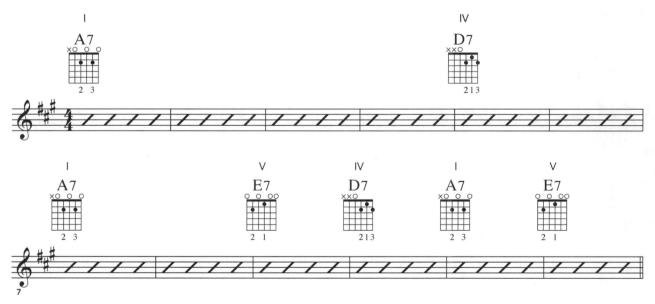

TIP: MANY TURNAROUNDS

We'll be playing the V chord for our turnarounds throughout this lesson, and they'll last one measure. But turnarounds can vary quite a bit in both their length and the chords they use. Some people stretch their turnarounds out to two measures, while others shrink them down to just half of the final measure. And more complicated chord progressions are sometimes substituted in place of just the V chord, as well, or by using a series of chords to lead into that V chord.

The "Quick IV"

The last variation we'll look at is the "quick IV" change. Along with a turnaround, this is the other most common change to the basic 12-bar blues form. Here, the "quick IV" refers to a quick change to the IV chord in measure 2 that moves back to the I for measures 3 and 4. This is how the 12-bar blues looks with a turnaround and a quick IV change:

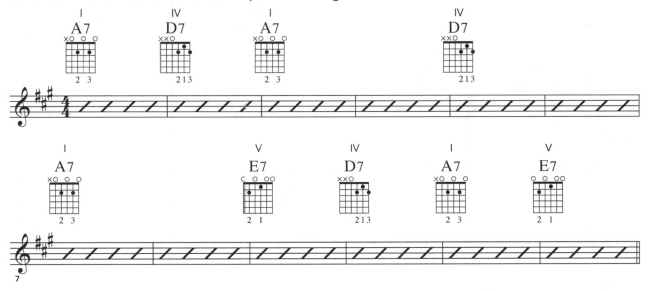

At this point, you have all the tools to back up somebody while they play the blues or to sing a blues song on your own! Now that we know how to play the blues in A, let's learn how to play it in some other keys.

The Blues in D

We also know enough chords to play the blues in D. Earlier in the book, we learned that the I, IV, and V chords in the key of D are D, G, and A, respectively. So if we just plug those chords into our blues progression, we get a blues in D:

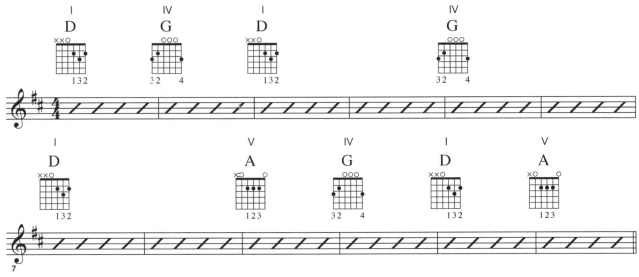

We almost know enough chords to play the blues in D using dominant seventh chords, too, since we know D7 and A7. But we don't know the G7, so let's learn how to play this chord, and then we can play the blues in D using dominant seventh chords.

THE G7 CHORD

To play a G7 chord, place your ring, middle, and index fingers on the sixth, fifth, and first strings, respectively. Your ring finger sits in the third-fret space, your middle finger sits in the second-fret space, and your index finger sits in the first-fret space. This is how a G7 chord looks:

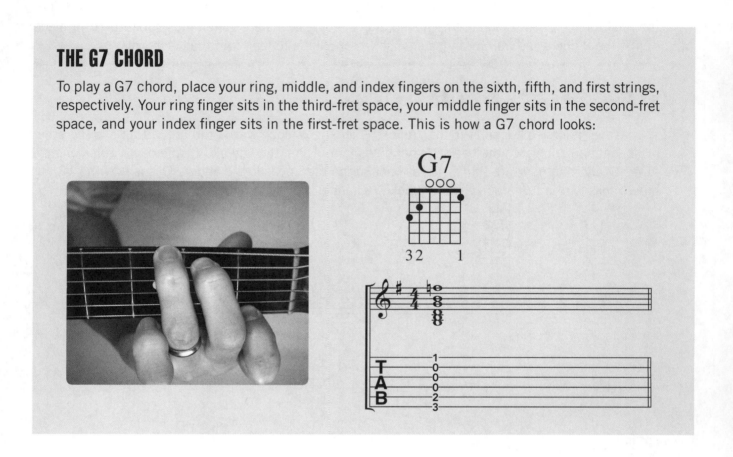

Now that we know G7, here's the blues in D using dominant seventh chords:

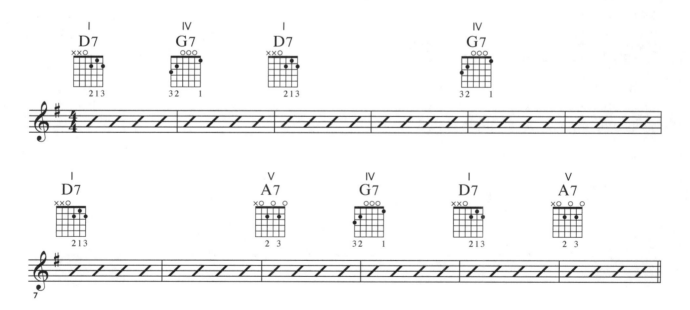

The Blues in G

At this point, we also know enough chords to play the blues in G using dominant seventh chords. In earlier chapters, we learned that the I IV, and V chords in the key of G are G, C, and D, respectively. So, using dominant seventh chords, our I, IV, and V chords will be G7 (I), C7 (IV), and D7 (V). Here's our blues in G with the quick V change and a turnaround:

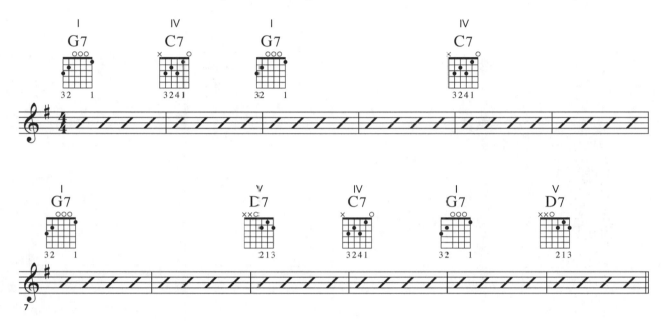

The Blues in E

Let's learn the blues in one more key, E, and you'll be able to jam with others on the blues in four different keys! The key of E is one of the most popular keys on the guitar, since the I chord, E, sounds so huge on a guitar. Before we map out our blues progression in E, let's figure out which chords we'll need. Since we're in the key of E, the I chord is E, and let's count up the scale to find the IV and V chords (hint: the key of E has four sharped notes—F#, C#, G#, and D#): E (1), F# (2), G# (3), A (4), B (5). So our I, IV, and V dominant seventh chords will be E7, A7, and B7, respectively.

But wait! We don't know how to play that B7 chord yet. So here it is:

THE B7 CHORD

To play a B7 chord, place your middle, ring, and pinky fingers on the second-fret space of the fifth, third, and first strings, respectively, then place your index finger in the first-fret space of the fourth string. This is how the B7 chord looks:

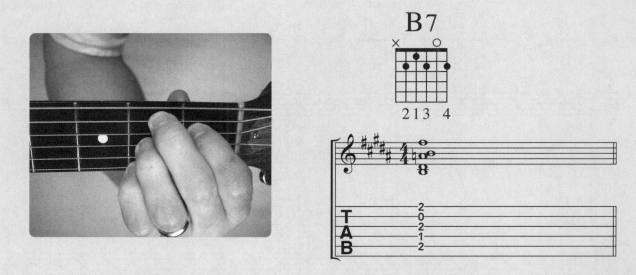

This four-fingered chord is quite hard to grab, so make sure each string sounds properly and adjust any fingers, if necessary.

Let's practice our B7 chord by placing it into our 12-bar blues in E. Here's how this progression looks with a quick IV change and a turnaround at the end:

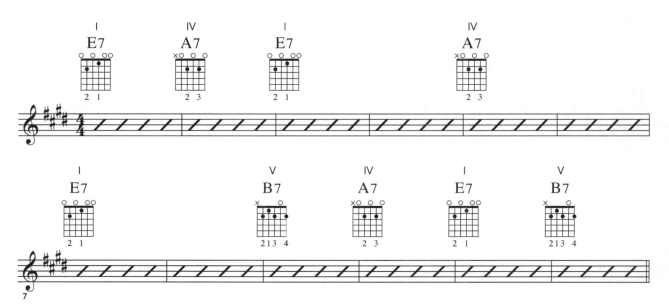

Now you're ready for a blues jam in E! Let's try out out the 12-bar blues in a song: "Dominant Seventh Blues."

TIP: THE PICKUP MEASURE AND THE FINAL MEASURE

Notice how the first measure in "Dominant Seventh Blues" isn't complete? There are only three eighth notes! This is another pickup measure (which we learned about in Chapter 6). If you don't remember what a pickup measure is, it's a few notes that lead into the beginning of a song, and they happen *before* the downbeat of the first measure. Since this pickup starts on the "and" of beat 3, simply count in "1-and, 2-and, 3-" and come in on the "and" of beat 3 (as shown underneath the music).

Also check out how the last measure of the song is in measure 13—not the 12th (and final) measure of the blues form. In many styles, including the blues, people often end the song by going back to the I chord after the very end of the form.

DOMINANT SEVENTH BLUES

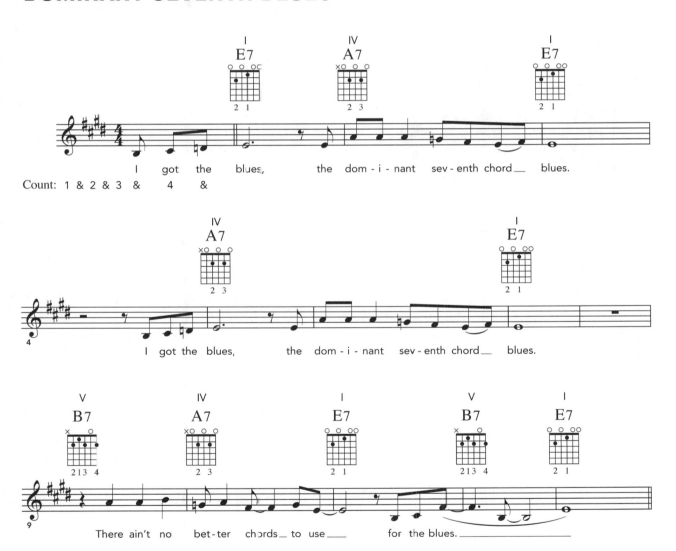

CHAPTER 12: THE F CHORD

The F chord is one of the more difficult chords to play, but you're ready to take it on! For all the chords we've learned so far, each finger on our fretting hand holds down one string. But with the F chord, you have to hold down *two* strings with one finger. To hold down two strings, you have to lay a finger flat on the fretboard, which is a technique called a *barre*. This is what makes it more difficult than other chords. Here's how to play the F chord:

THE F CHORD

To play an F chord, place your ring finger on the third-fret space of the fourth string and your middle finger on the second-fret space of the third string. Then barre your index finger across the top two strings at the first fret ("barre" means to flatten your finger across more than one string so that you fret multiple strings with one finger). This is how an F chord looks:

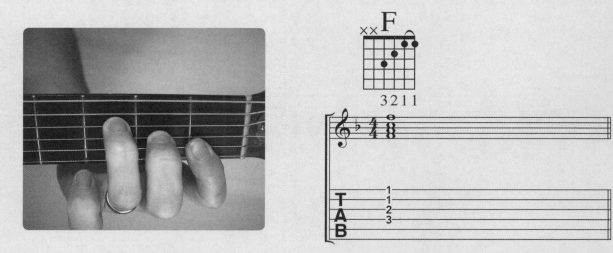

This is one of the hardest chords we've played, since you have to fret every note of the chord, and you have to barre across the top two strings with your index finger. Because of this, don't worry if you need extra time to get this chord under your fingers. Make sure to strum slowly through the chord to help detect any buzzing, and—if you find it—readjust your fingers so that the frets don't buzz.

Now let's work the F chord into a chord progression. The F chord is the IV chord in the key of C, so let's try this out in a I–IV–V progression in the key of C. First, let's find out what our V chord is, so we'll count up the scale from C: C (1), D (2), E (3), F (4), G (5). So our I–IV–V will be C–F–G. Here it is, using a simple strumming pattern so you can practice fretting that F chord and not worry too much about what your picking hand is doing:

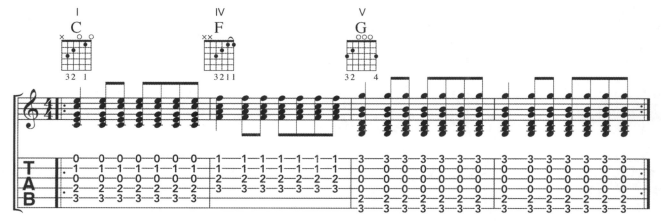

Now let's try an alternate-bass strumming pattern with our F chord. An easy way to do this is to alternate between the fourth and third strings, like this:

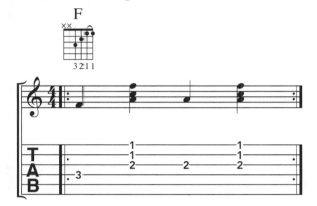

Let's try this in our I–IV–V progression in C. Here's one way we could do that:

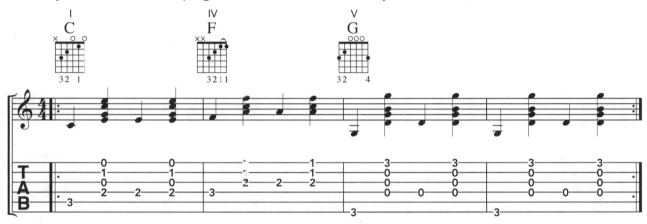

If you want a lower bass note for the F chord, you could reach down with your ring finger to grab the third fret of the fifth string on beat 3. This is a similar move to what we did with C and C7 chords:

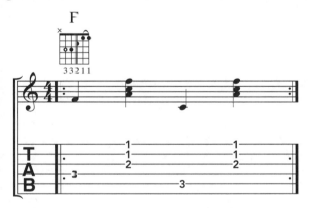

Now let's try this move out in our I–IV–V progression in C. Let's change the bass notes for the C chord, as well, for variety:

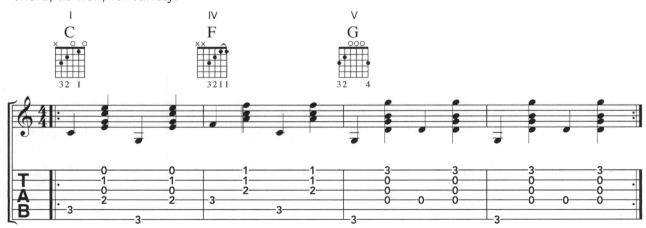

The F Chord in the Blues

We already know that in the key of C, our I, IV, and V chords are C, F, and G. Let's plug those chords into a blues progression now, giving us one more key in which to play the blues. Let's use the quick IV change along with a turnaround in the final measure:

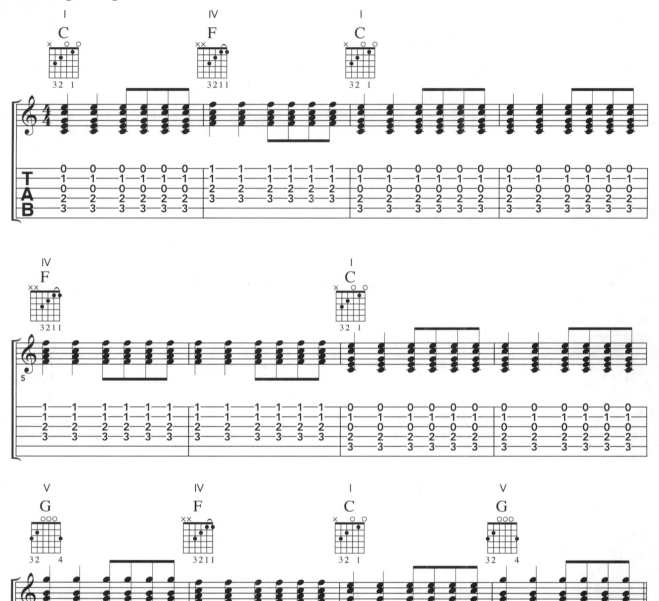

To play our blues using dominant seventh chords, we'll need to know how to play an F7 chord:

THE F7 CHORD

To play an F7 chord, place your ring finger on the third-fret space of the fourth string and your middle finger on the second-fret space of the third string. Then add your pinky finger to the fourth-fret space of the second string and your index finger to the first-fret space of the first string.

This is how an F7 chord looks:

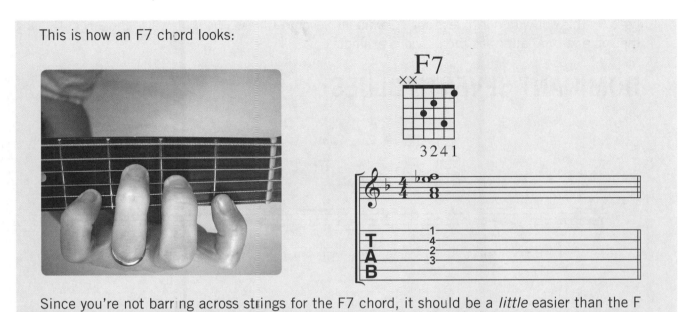

Since you're not barring across strings for the F7 chord, it should be a *little* easier than the F chord. Still, take your time with it strum slowly through the chord to help detect any buzzing, and—if you find it—readjust your fingers so that the frets don't buzz.

Now we're ready for our 12-bar blues in C using dominant seventh chords:

Let's try this out with our blues tune "Dominant Seventh Blues." We'll play it in the key of C using the same strum pattern as the previous example:

DOMINANT SEVENTH BLUES

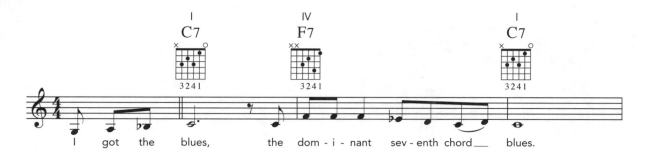

I got the blues, the dom - i - nant sev - enth chord___ blues.

I got the blues, the dom - i - nant sev - enth chord___ blues.

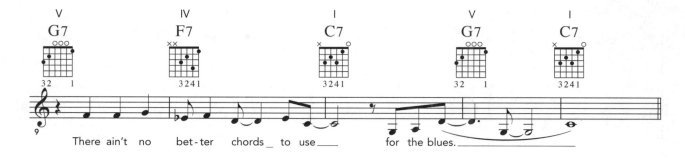

There ain't no bet - ter chords _ to use___ for the blues.___

CHAPTER 13: SIXTEENTH-NOTE STRUM PATTERNS

So far, we've played strum patterns that use quarter notes and eighth notes. As we've seen, quarter notes are twice as long as eighth notes, meaning that you can fit two eighth notes in every quarter-note beat. But what happens when you split an eighth note in two? You get a *sixteenth note*. You can fit two sixteenth notes in each eighth note, which means that you can fit *four* sixteenth notes in each quarter note—or four in each beat. To fit all these strums in, you'll have to move your hand twice as fast. That means that, for each quarter-note pulse, your hand will move down and up *twice*, instead of just once. Let's try this out by strumming steady sixteenth notes. Count along by saying "One-ee-and-ah, two-ee-and-ah, three-ee-and-ah, four-ee-and-ah."

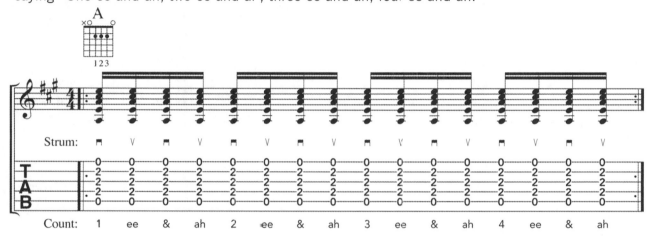

Let's get comfortable with strumming sixteenth notes by plugging these strums into some of our chord progressions. Here's a I–IV–V progression in the key of A using sixteenth notes:

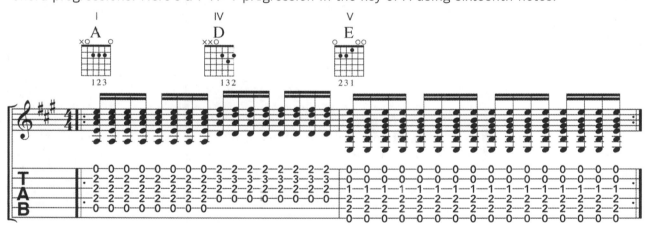

And here's a ii–V–I progression in the key of D that uses a sixteenth-note strum pattern:

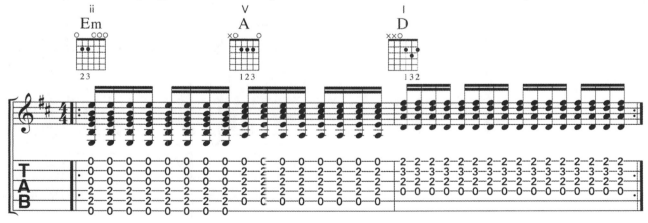

Syncopated Sixteenth Notes

Just as we did with eighth notes, we can vary our sixteenth-note strum patterns as well. If we leave out the first downstroke on beats 2 and 4, we have a syncopated pattern that sounds a little less frenetic than strumming steady sixteenth notes:

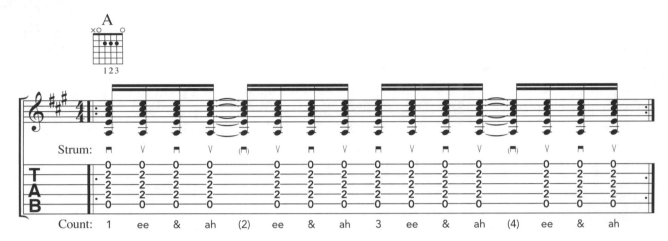

Count along and remember that your pick will still move down on beats 2 and 4 (but won't connect with the strings, instead strumming through the air). Let's hear how this sounds in a I–IV–V progression:

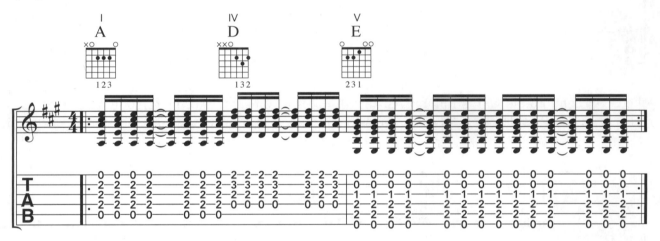

You can also mix eighth notes in with your sixteenth-note strum patterns. Let's try one that uses eighth notes on beats 1 and 3 and sixteenth notes on beats 2 and 4. Pay attention to the pick direction markings. Since your arm is moving twice as fast for these sixteenth notes, you'll be playing all downstrokes for the eighth notes on beats 1 and 3:

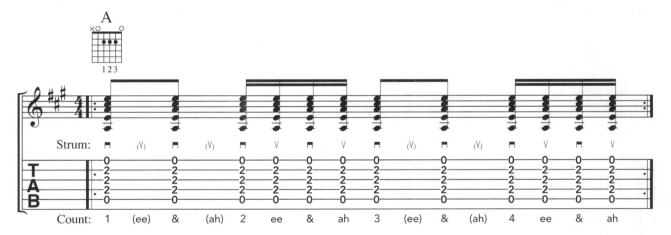

Now let's try playing just *one* eighth-note strum on beats 1 and 3, filling in the rest of each beat with sixteenth notes:

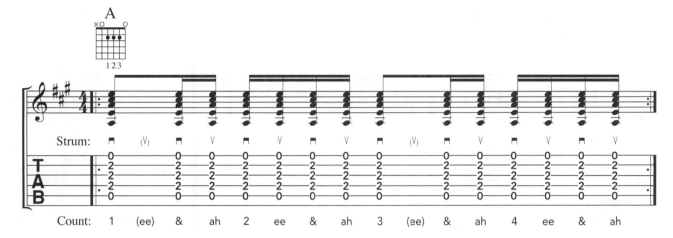

You can play syncopated patterns that include both eighth and sixteenth notes, as well. Let's use the pattern from our last example, but leave out the strums on beats 2 and 4 to create a nice syncopated pattern.

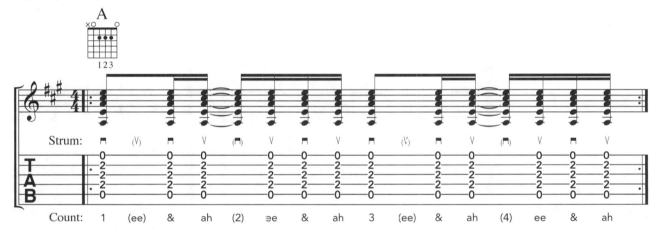

Bass-Note Strums with Sixteenth Notes

Let's try adding sixteenth notes to our bass-note strums. We'll start with a quarter-note bass note on beats 1 and 3, filling out the rest of the measure with sixteenth notes. With such a long pause between the quarter note and the following sixteenth notes, it can be easy to lose the rhythm, so remember to keep your hand moving down and up with the sixteenth-note subdivision by just strumming "through the air" in front of the strings after each quarter note until the next following sixteenth note:

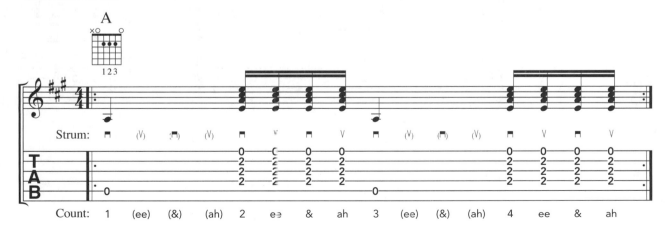

Now let's try an eighth note on beats 1 and 3 and fill everything else in with sixteenth notes:

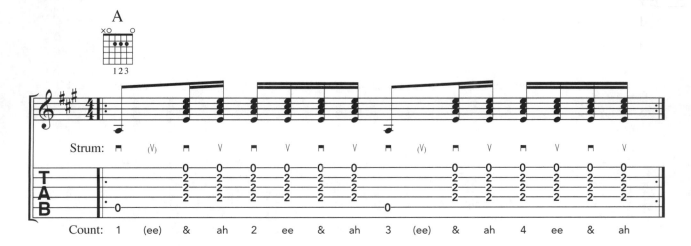

And we can syncopate this, as well. Let's try leaving out the downstrokes on beats 2 and 4:

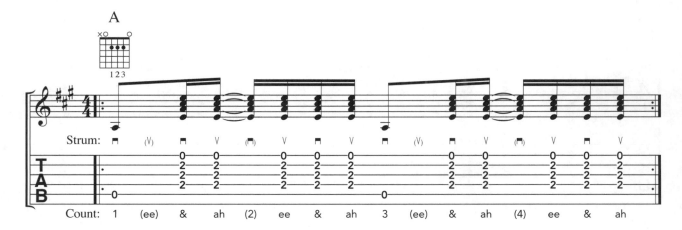

Try this pattern out with a ii–V–I progression in G to get this motion into your arm and fingers:

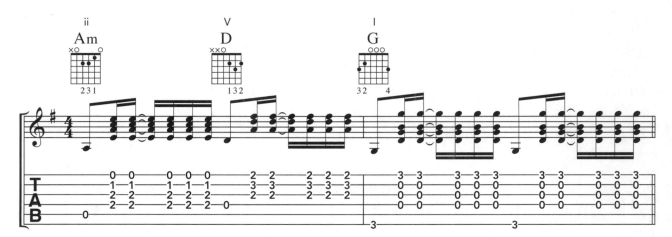

Alternate-Bass Strumming with Sixteenth Notes

We can also inject our alternate-bass strumming with a sixteenth-note pulse. Here, it's very similar to the way alternate-bass strumming sounds with eighth notes—it's just twice as quick! We'll play a bass note on *every* beat, like this:

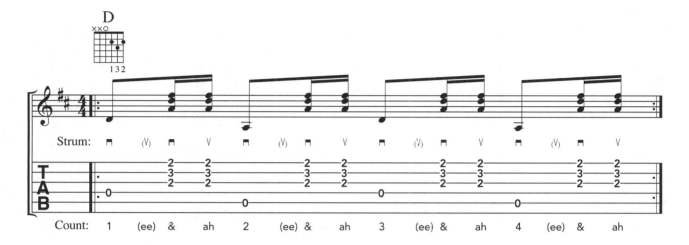

TIP: THE STRUMS FOR ALTERNATE-BASS STRUMMING

You may notice that sometimes the alternate-bass strums are shown on just the top three strings, but other times they may show four or more strings. Don't worry too much about *how many* strings you're strumming; just make sure you're strumming part of the chord. Generally, people strum the top portions of the chord, leaving out the lowest note or notes (which are covered by the bass note pluck).

Let's take this ultra-quick alternate-bass strumming for a spin on a I–IV–V progression in the key of D:

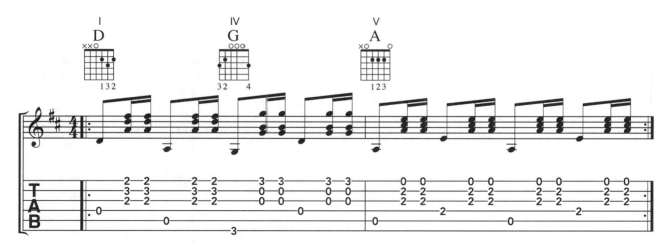

Now let's try it out on a I–IV–V in the key of C. Don't worry if that F chord slows you down! That just means you need a little more practice with it. Remember to slow down the example to a speed at which you can play it through cleanly. Then, gradually speed it up until you can play it at the speed you want to.

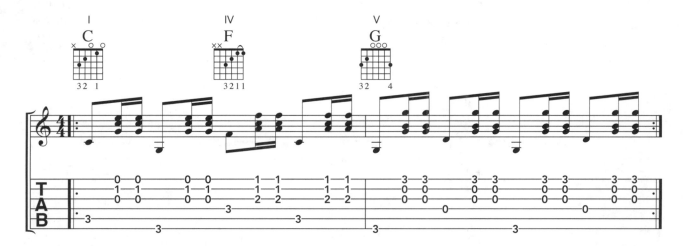

We'll finish this lesson off by playing our quick alternate-bass strumming patterns in a couple of ii–V–I progressions. The first one is in the key of C, and the second one is in the key of G:

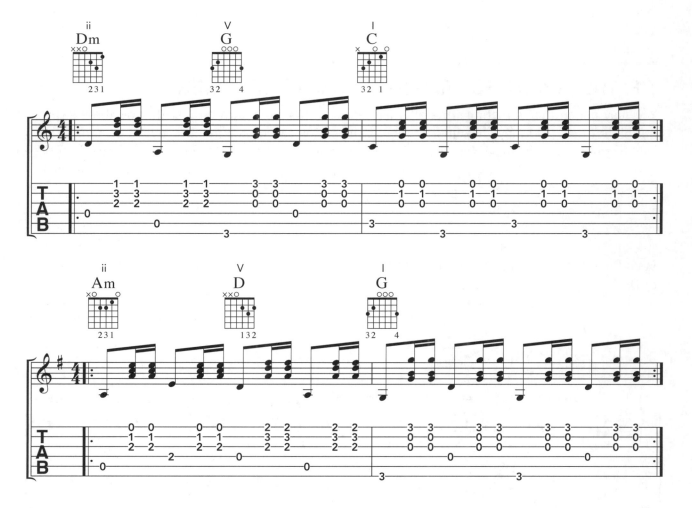

CHAPTER 14: MORE MAJOR KEY PROGRESSIONS

In this chapter, we'll learn two more classic pop and rock progressions: the I–vi–ii–V progression and the I–♭VII–IV progression. These two progressions alone account for countless songs from the '50s through the current day. While we're learning these progressions, we'll also work on expanding our sixteenth-note strum patterns and learn how to play with a different type of rhythm as well!

The I–Vi–ii–V Progression

As the name states, the I–vi–ii–V progression works with the I, ii, V, and vi chords. Since we've already worked with the I, ii, and V chords before, the vi chord is the only new chord in this progression. As you'd expect, you can find the vi chord by walking up the scale to the sixth degree. We'll start by learning a I–vi–ii–V progression in the key of C, so let's count up through the sixth degree of the C scale to find our ii, V, and vi chords (the key of C has no sharped or flatted notes): C (1), D (2), E (3), F (4), G (5), A (6). Since the V chord is uppercase, it's major—a G chord. And since the ii and vi chord are lowercase, they'll be minor—Dm and Am, respectively. So that gives us C–Am–Dm–G for our I–vi–ii–V progression. Let's play it with a steady strum pattern using a quarter note followed by eighth notes:

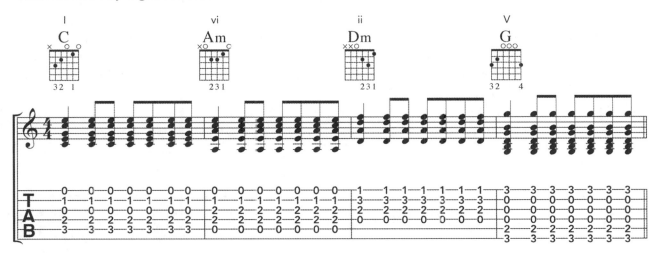

Now let's try switching chords every two beats using quarter-note strums followed by two eighth-note strums for each chord. If you're playing it slowly enough, it should sound similar to dozens of '50s hits, like "Earth Angel."

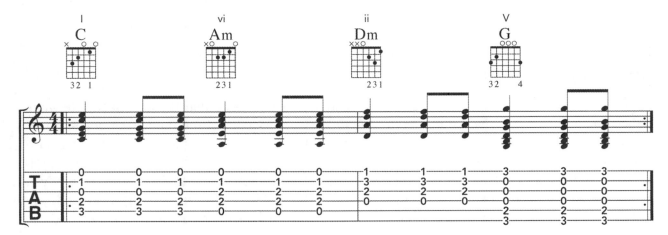

Now let's teach ourselves how to play a I–vi–ii–V progression in the key of G. Since we're in the key of G, we know that G is the I chord. Let's find the other chords by walking up the scale (hint: the G has one sharped note—F♯—but we won't reach it): G (1), A (2), B (3), C (4), D (5), E (6). So, our major V chord is D, and our minor ii and vi chords are Am and Em, respectively. Let's try out our new I–vi–ii–v progression:

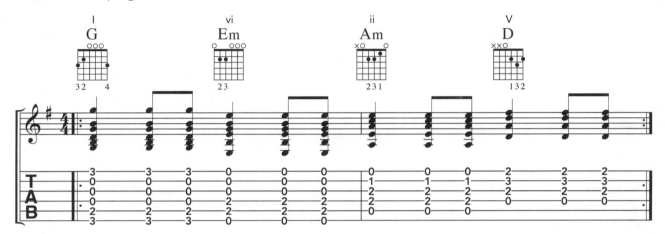

6/8 Time

The I–vi–ii–V progression is a great one to play in 6/8 time. If you want to know more about 6/8 time, take a look at the nearby tip, but all you *really* need to know is that instead of there being four beats per measure—like we're used to—now there are *six* beats per measure. The other key thing is that, instead of a quarter note getting a beat, now an *eighth note gets a beat*. Let's try playing our I–vi–ii–V progression using eighth-note strums in the key of C. Here, we'll play steady eighth-note strums, and we'll play each of these strums with a downstroke. As you play, accent beats 1 and 4. So if you count along, do the same: **1** 2 3, **4** 5 6.

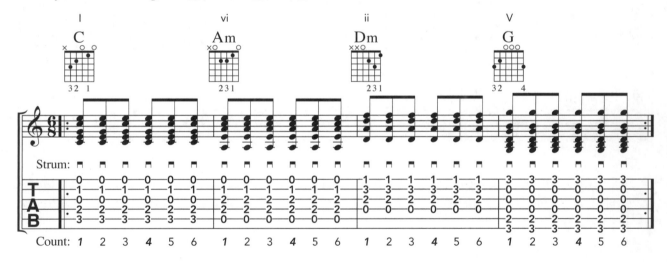

TIP: TIME SIGNATURES

Time signatures tell us two things: how many beats we have in each measure and what note value gets counted as a beat. The top number in the time signature tells us the number of beats. So, in 4/4 time, the 4 on top tells us that we have 4 beats; in 6/8 time, the 6 on top tells us that we have 6 beats. The *bottom* note tells us what note value gets a beat. This is slightly trickier than the top number, but think of it as a fraction with the number on the top being "1." So, in 4/4 time, you put a "1" on top of the fraction, then take the "4" from the bottom of the time signature and you get ¼—so a quarter note gets one beat. In 6/8 time, use "1" again on top of the fraction and the "8" on the bottom and you get 1/8—an eighth note gets a beat.

Now let's add some sixteenth notes to our 6/8 strum pattern. Let's play the sixteenth notes on beats 2 and 3 of each measure, and we'll use upstrokes for the second of each pair of sixteenth notes. Remember to keep your arm moving up and down.

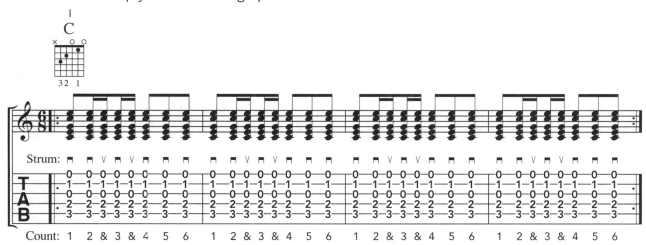

Do you recognize that pattern now? This is another extremely common sound as the backbone of many hits. Now let's try our new strum pattern in a I–vi–ii–V progression in the key of C:

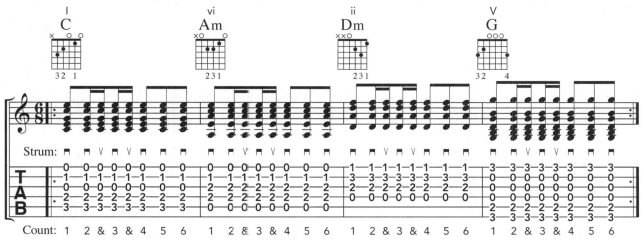

More Sixteenth-Note Strum Patterns

So far, we've gotten comfortable playing sixteenth-note strum patterns and mixing them up with eighth note strums. But you can mix sixteenth-note strums with any type of strum. Let's try alternating between a quarter-note strum and four sixteenth-note strums, using our I–vi–ii–V progression in C:

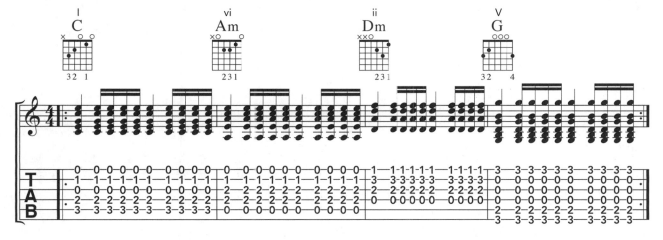

Of course, we can add eighth-note strums in as well. This next one's starting to get pretty tricky, so make sure to count along!

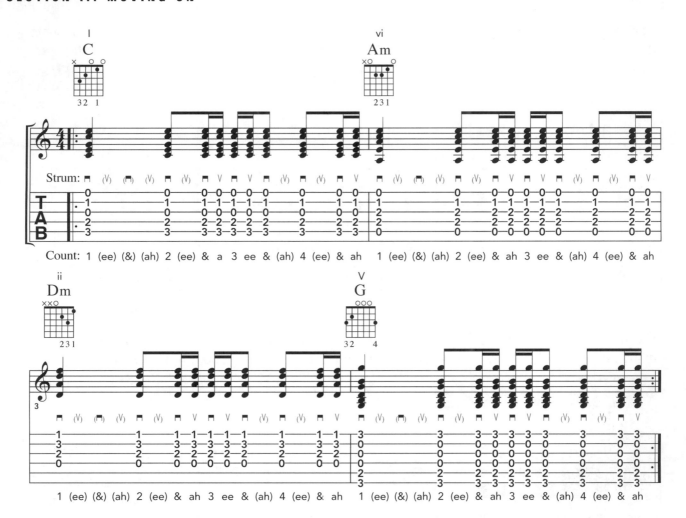

When we add syncopation to this, we can get some pretty funky and cool strum patterns. (Remember to slow this one down, too, and count if you have problems!)

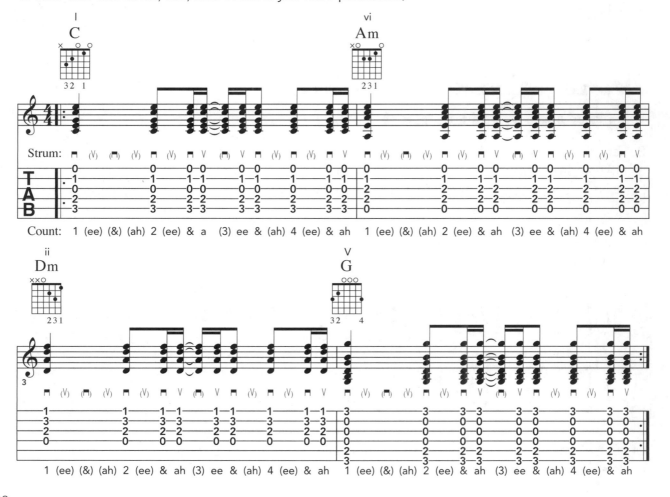

The I–♭VII–IV Progression

Another extremely popular classic rock progression uses the ♭VII chord between the I and IV chords. We're not going to worry too much about the theory of the ♭VII chord. (*If you'd like to know a little more about the ♭VII chord, see the nearby sidebar on "The ♭VII Chord and Finding the I–♭VII–IV Progression."*) We'll start out with a I–♭VII–IV chord in the key of D, which is D–C–G.

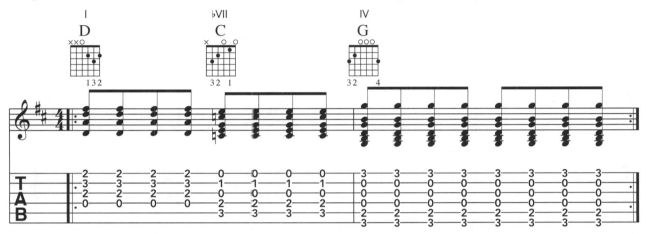

THE ♭VII CHORD AND FINDING THE I–♭VII–IV PROGRESSION

You can find the ♭VII chord by counting backwards down the scale one degree from the I chord. The "flat" means that we'll actually flatten the lettername of the chord we reach when we count down the scale. Don't worry, as this isn't too complicated. Let's try this out in the key of D. Starting at D, we'll count one note backwards to C♯ (the key of D has two sharped notes: F♯ and C♯). Then we'll flatten that C♯ to C (or lower it by a *half step*; *steps*, or *intervals* are distances between notes—a half step is a one-fret distance on the guitar, while a *whole step* is a two-fret distance—*learn more about this in the* Appendix). So C is our ♭VII chord. In the key of D, we know we can count up to the fourth degree to find the IV chord, so let's do that now (hint: remember that there are two sharps in the key of D—F♯ and C♯): D (1), E (2), F♯ (3), G (4). So G is our IV chord, and that means our I–♭VII–IV progression is D–C–G in the key of D.

The ♭VII chord occurs naturally in minor keys. When we use it in a major chord progression, we're "borrowing" it from the minor key with the same letter name. (*For more on minor key chord functions, see the* Appendix.)

You likely recognize this progression as the backbone to classic rock tunes like "Sweet Home Alabama" and many others. Let's try a syncopated sixteenth-note strum pattern out over our I–♭VII–IV progression, and we can make it sound even more like the rhythm to "Sweet Home Alabama." This one's tricky, and it's the first time we've created syncopation by leaving out the "and" upstrokes (in the middle of beats 2 and 4). Make sure to count along and keep that arm moving steadily up and down!

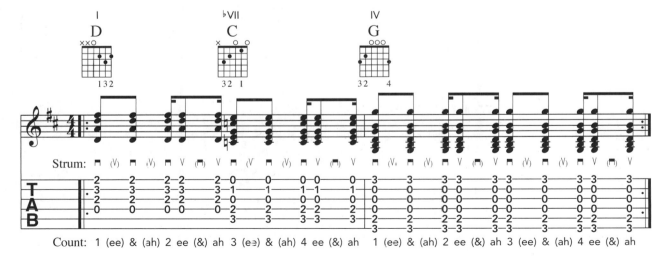

TIP: AN EASY WAY TO FIND THE ♭VII

You can find the ♭VII on your guitar without having to count up or down scale degrees. Simply find the letter note of the key you're in (for instance, start on D if you're in the key of D), and then find the note two frets lower than that note; that's the root of your ♭VII chord! In this case, the note C is two frets lower than a D note, so a C chord is the ♭VII in the key of D.

Let's learn this progression in the key of E, which is E–D–A:

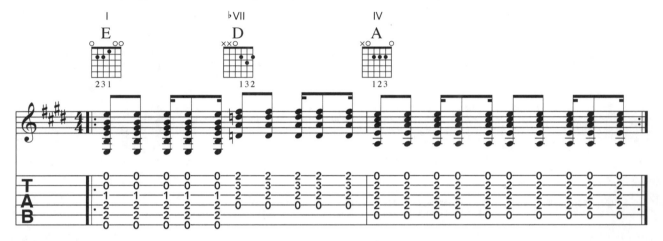

FINDING THE I–♭VII–IV IN THE KEY OF E

Since E is the key, it'll be the I chord, and counting backwards one degree gives us D♯ (the key of E has four sharps: F♯, C♯, D♯, and G♯). We'll then flatten that to D for the ♭VII chord. Now let's count up to the fourth degree to find our IV chord: E (1), F♯ (2), G♯ (3), A (4). So A is the IV chord, and that means our I–♭VII–IV progression is E–D–A in the key of E.

This progression sounds huge in E, so feel free to play it for a while! Once you're done, let's try it in the key of A. Here, our I–♭VII–IV progression will be A–G–D:

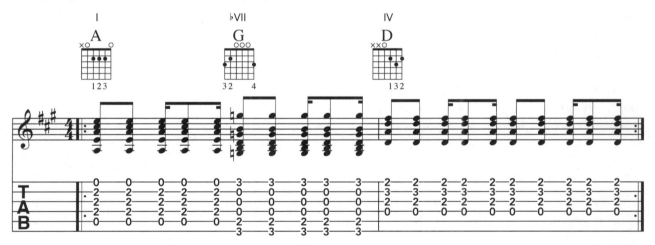

FINDING THE I–♭VII–IV IN THE KEY OF A

A will be the I chord, and the key of A has three sharps: F♯, C♯, and G♯. Counting back one degree from A gives us G♯, which we then flatten to G for the ♭VII chord. Next, we'll count up to the fourth degree for the IV chord: A (1), B (2), C♯ (3), D (4). So our IV chord is D, and our I–♭VII–IV progression in the key of A is A–G–D.

Let's learn this progression in one more key—the key of G. Here, our I–♭VII–IV is G–F–C:

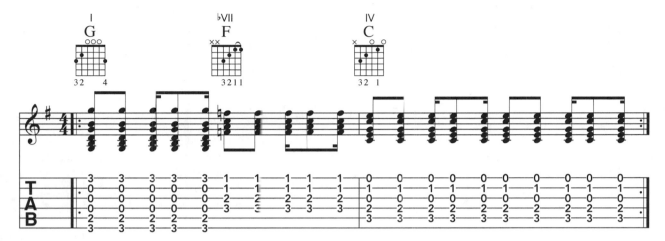

FINDING THE I–♭VII–IV IN THE KEY OF G

G will be the I chord, and it has only one sharp: F♯. So counting back one degree gives us F♯, which we'll flatten to F for the ♭VII chord. Now let's find the IV chord: G (1), A (2), B (3), C (4). So C is the IV chord, and our I–♭VII–IV progression in G is G–F–C.

You might need to spend a little extra time on this one, since that F chord is our newest chord. Feel free to slow it down and use a metronome if you need to. Once you're comfortable at a slower pace, you can gradually speed it up to the tempo I'm playing it at on the video.

Thumping Bass Strums

We've strummed chords and played bass notes, but another way to give your songs a rhythmic jolt is to mix these two concepts together by playing the bottom two or three strings of a chord, then strumming through the complete chord to contrast those thumping bassy strums. Let's try this out using our I–♭VII–IV progression in the key of E. We'll strum through the bottom set of strings on beats 1 and 3 (for both eighth notes in each pair), then strum through the whole chord for every strum on beats 2 and 4, like this:

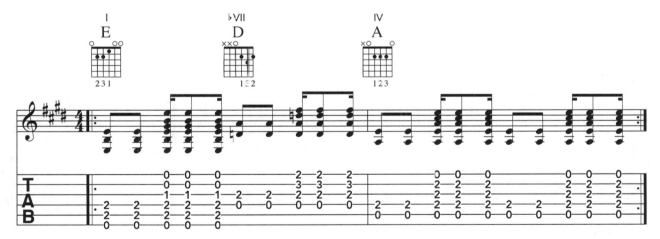

Don't worry about how many strings you hit for the bassy strums—one, two, or three strings should all work fine—but find what sounds best to you. You can add even more of a thumping sound by slapping the palm of your picking hand into the strings as you pluck those low bass notes—a technique called *palm muting*.

We'll finish this chapter off with a song using our new thumping bass strums along with a I–♭VII–IV progression. But first, let's add a sixteenth note to our strum pattern on beats 2 and 4. This makes the pattern a little easier and will make it less confusing when we try singing over the top of it. You can play the syncopated pattern later, if you like. Here's our new pattern:

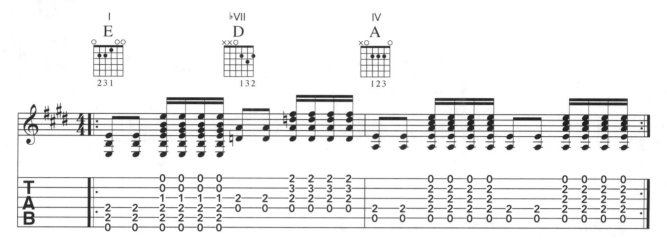

And here's our song: "Home to Alaska." For that classic rock sound, try adding in some palm muting to the bass-like strums on beats 1 and 3 in each measure.

HOME TO ALASKA

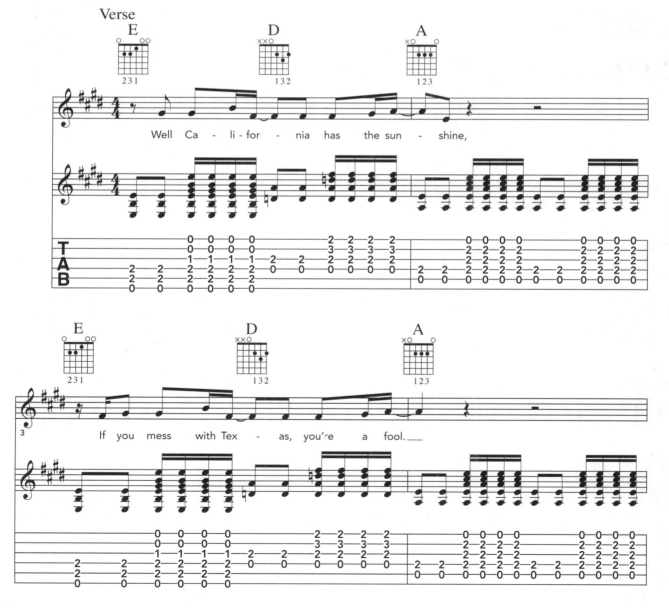

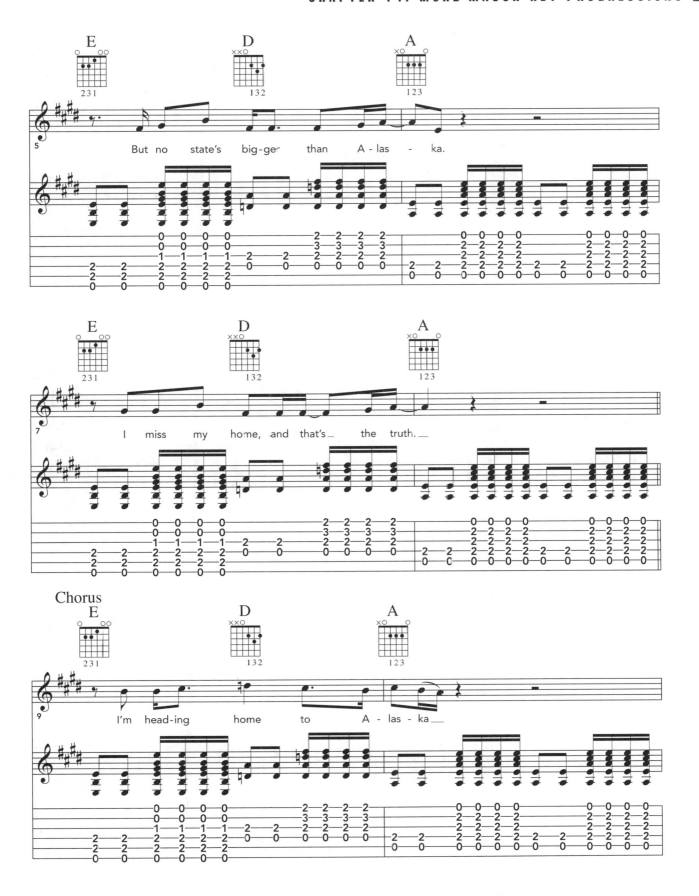

But no state's big-ger than A - las - ka.

I miss my home, and that's the truth.

Chorus

I'm head-ing home to A - las - ka

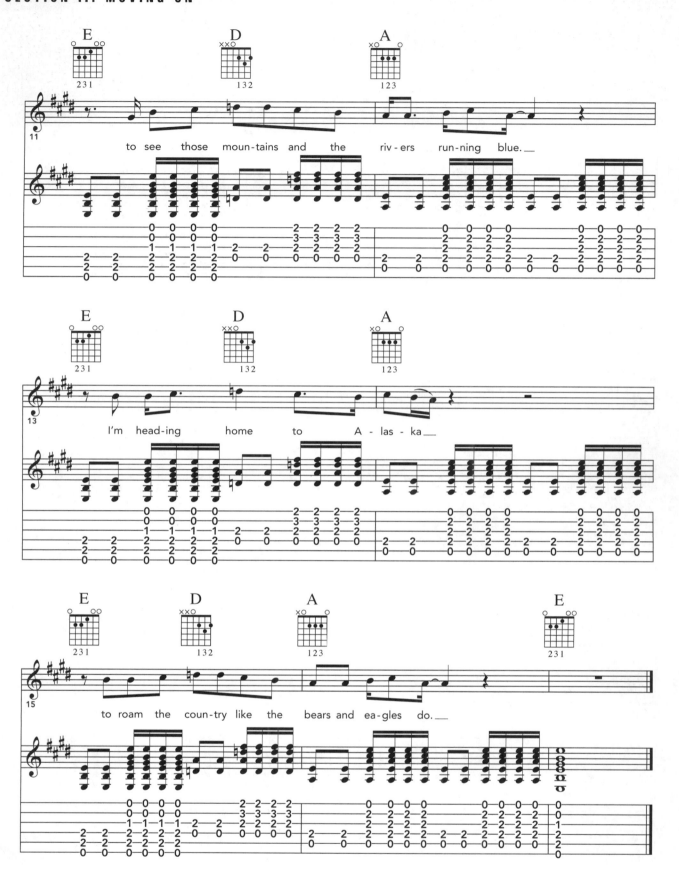

CHAPTER 15: WALKING BASS LINES

When you want to add a little interest to your strum patterns, one great way is by adding *walking bass lines*—single notes that join chords in a progression. They work great for any kind of strum pattern and especially well for bass-note strums and alternate-bass strumming.

Let's start by playing a G–C chord progression:

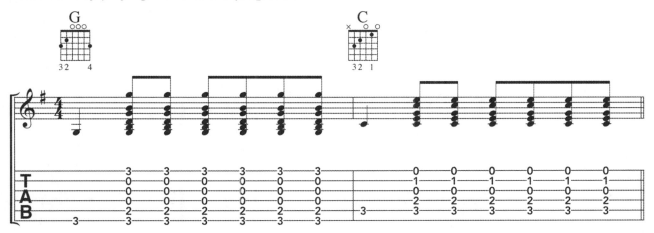

Now, instead of playing the strums on beats 3 and 4 of the first measure, we'll play single notes that walk up to the C note on the downbeat of the next measure:

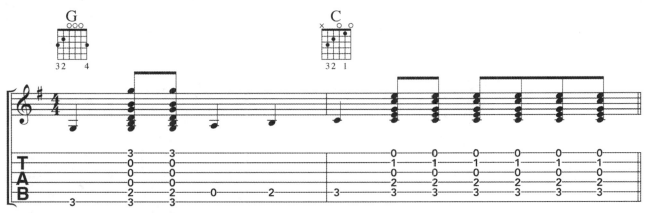

Let's see how this sounds in a I–IV–V progression in the key of G, and here we'll try it with alternate-bass strums:

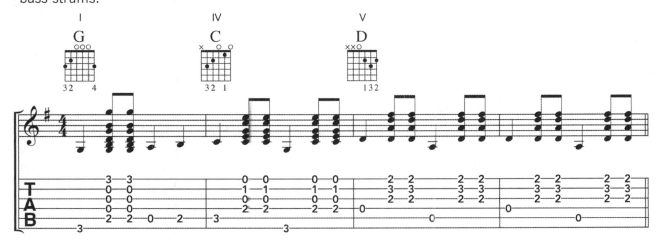

To get from the G chord to the C chord, we walk up, but we can also walk *down*. Let's try playing a repeated G–C progression, and this time we'll walk down to that G chord from the C chord:

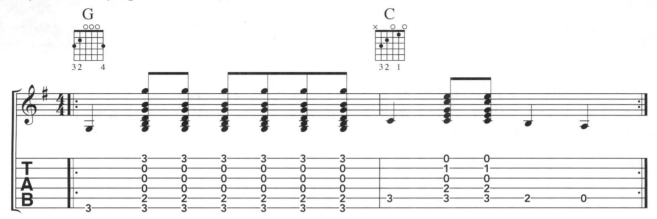

You can even do *both* up and down. Here's our G–C progression with a walking bass line going up from G to C and another one walking down from C back to G:

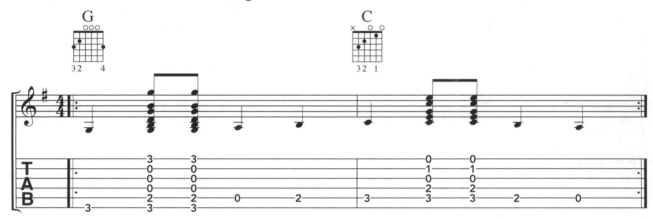

Now let's try walking down in a I–♭VII–IV progression in G to hear how this sounds in one of our newer progressions. Let's play alternate-bass strums with this one:

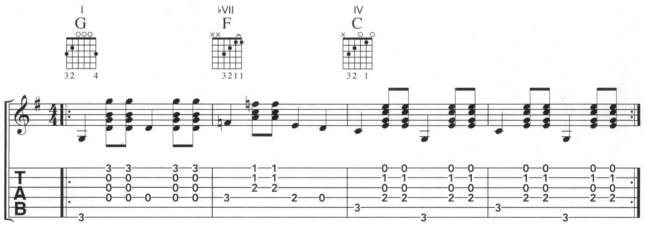

TIP: HOW DO I KNOW WHICH NOTES TO USE?

When you're coming up with your own walking bass lines, a good rule of thumb is that if you use notes from the scale affiliated with the key you're in, they'll sound fine. (*For more on keys and scales, see the* Appendix.) If you don't know how to find the major or minor scales to use, then simply use your ear. Try walking through a few notes, and if they sound good—great! If they don't sound good, try and pinpoint the bad-sounding one and then move that note up or down a fret. Eventually, you'll find a set of notes that sound good to your years; and if it sounds good to you, then it *is* good!

We can walk through almost any chord in a progression. Let's try our I–IV–V progression again. This time, we'll again walk up from the G chord to the C chord, but we'll also walk down from the D chord back to the G chord:

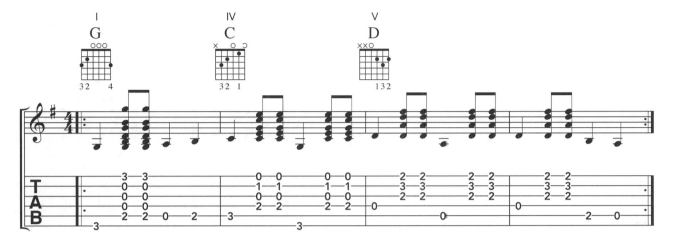

Did you notice that here we walked down from D to G through the same notes as we did from the C chord? Our D chord is higher than a C chord, so if we were going to walk all the way down from D to G, we could go through all these notes:

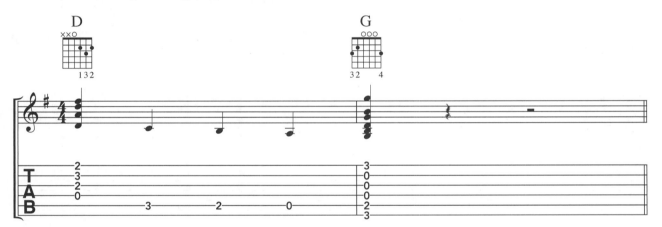

But this run starts on beat 3, and we don't have enough time in our strum pattern to do that! So, we just leave out the first note. In general, when you're leaving out notes, it's best to focus on the ones you're leaving *in*, making sure you keep notes that lead right into the next chord. For instance, here we're keeping the notes that move into the G chord (more important) and omitting a note that's closer to the D chord—the chord we're moving *from*.

Of course, if we *did* have more space in our progression to move from D back to G, we could play all the notes in between. For instance, we could start our bass run on beat 1, like this:

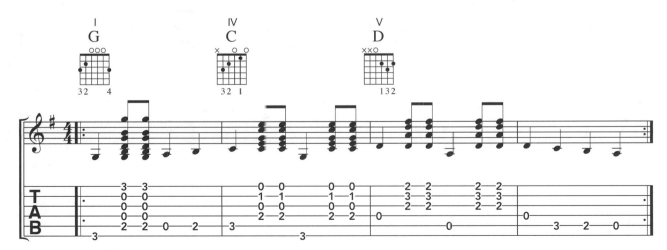

Now let's try a walking bass line in a ii–V–I progression in G (Am–D–G). Here, we can use the same walk down from D to G that we used in the I–IV–V, but we'll be adding a new one between the Am and D chords:

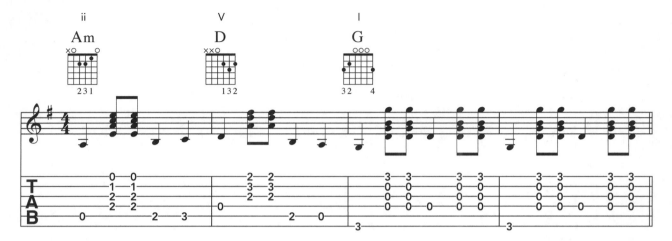

You can play these walking bass lines between most any chord, and you can play them in any key. For instance, let's try a walking bass line between an A and a D chord:

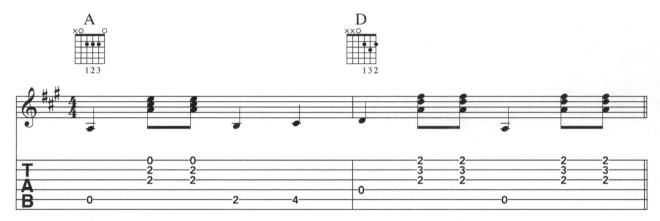

Here, we'll play a I–IV–V progression in the key of A (A–D–E), and we'll use walking bass lines between the A and D chords and E and A chords (on the return from E to A again).

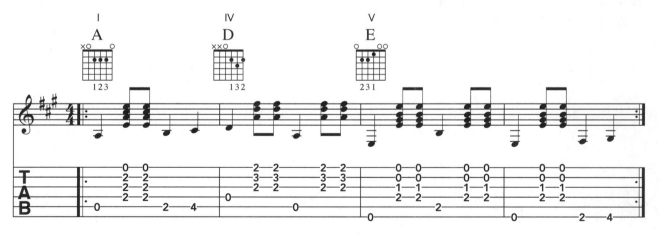

Let's try those walking bass lines in a ii–V–I progression in the key of D (Em–A–D):

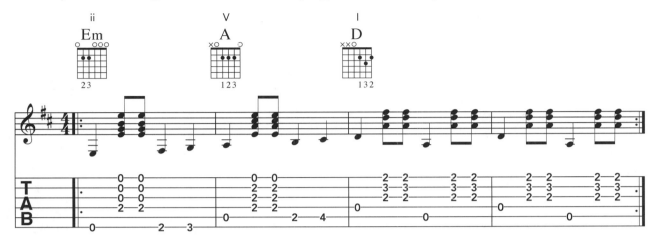

Notice how we walked *up* from the A (V) to the D (I) chord? Earlier in the chapter, we played walking bass lines with a ii–V–I in the key of G. Since the V chord (D) had a higher bass note than the I chord (G), we walked *down* from the V to the I. But in the key of D, our V chord (A) has a *lower* bass note than our I chord (D), so we can walk up to the I chord in this context.

CHROMATIC WALKING BASS LINES

A *chromatic* note is any note that's not part of the scale you're in. Your ear will usually tell you when you hit a chromatic note, because it usually doesn't sound right with the chords you're playing. But sometimes a chromatic note in a bass run can sound pretty good. For instance, we can wedge an extra note in our walk from G to C if we want to. That extra note (the B♭), is a chromatic note:

This sounds fine in the context of our bass run, doesn't it? This also makes the bass run a little longer, which means it will fit in a different space than our other walk from G to C—handy for fitting different songs.

As you come up with your own walking bass lines, experiment with the notes you choose. Sometimes you'll come across chromatic notes, and sometimes they'll work (of course, sometimes they won't!). But, as we talked about already in this lesson, let your ear tell you what works and doesn't work; your ear will know.

Adding Strums Between Bass Notes

We've learned how to play walking bass lines as single-note runs that connect chords, but we can also alternate the notes of our walking bass lines with chord strums. For instance, to move from a G to a C chord, we could play it as shown in the following example. We'll go back to a bass-note strum pattern so you can see the bass line a little more easily.

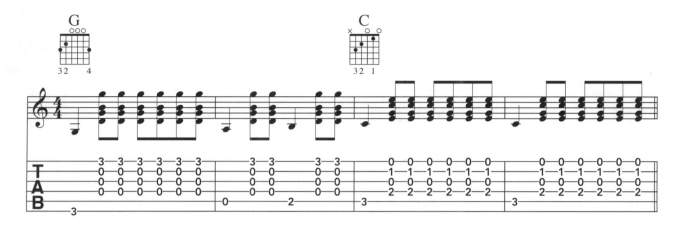

Notice how it takes a little more time to walk between the chords, since we're playing strums in between each bass note? This gives a different feel to a song, but it's also an effective way of creating motion as you move between chords. One thing to keep in mind is that, since it takes a different amount of time to move from one chord to another, you'll need more room for these types of walking bass lines. Now let's add a walking bass line from C back to the G chord:

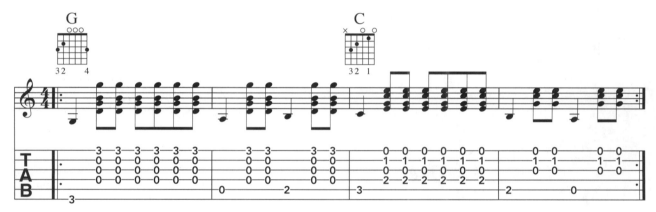

When you play the B note (the first note of the fourth measure), you have to move your middle finger down from the fourth string to play that note. That means that the note on the fourth string isn't really part of a C chord anymore, and that's why I've written it so you don't strum through that string during the fourth measure. But in many real-world cases, we may accidentally hit that string, and it won't usually matter—especially if the tempo is on the quicker side. Here's how that section sounds if we do strum through the fourth string:

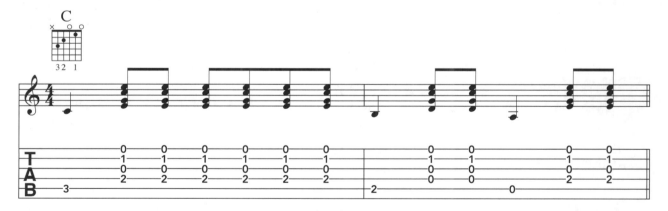

It may sound a little strange on its own, but in the context of other chords and the moving bass lines, it doesn't sound all that bad. This is good to know as you come up with your own moving bass lines, especially in places like moving from a D chord back to a G chord, as shown in the following example. You'll need to reach down with your pinky to get the C bass note on beat 3 of measure 1. Then, on beat 1 of measure 2, you have to remove your index finger from the third string and move it down to the fourth string to grab that B note.

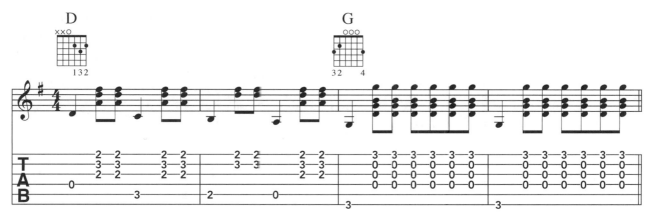

Notice how I've left out the third string for the strum on beat 2 of measure 2. Since your index finger moved down to the fifth string, it's no longer holding down its note on the third string, so that third string is not part of a D chord anymore. But again, it doesn't sound too bad if you *do* play this note, as we see in the next example:

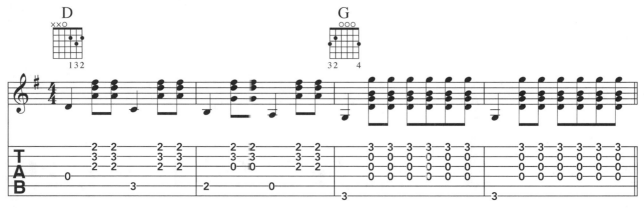

In both of the previous two examples, move your index finger *back* to the third string as you play the open A bass note on beat 3 of measure 2, as this allows you to play the full D chord on beat 4.

Now let's put these bass lines into the context of a I–IV–V progression in the key of G, so we can hear them in action:

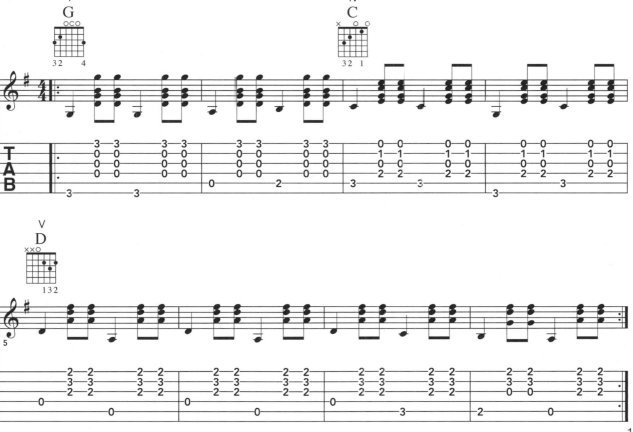

Notice how I had to stretch our I–IV–V progression out to eight measures to fit in those runs. Also check out how I pause on the C bass note in measure 3, then use alternate-bass strumming in measure 4. I wanted to mirror the bass motion from the G chord (measure 1) over to the C chord in measure 4, but wanted the forward momentum of the alternate bass in measure 4.

Remember that you can come up with walking bass lines in any key. Let's try it now for a I–IV–V progression in the key of D (D–G–A):

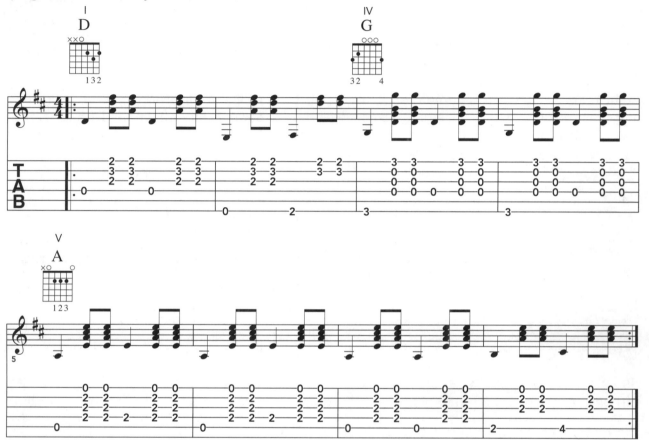

Notice how here I go all the way down to the low E string to play the walkup into the G chord. We have one more walking bass line here—from the A chord back up to the D chord.

Now come up with some walking bass lines of your own. Use some of the progressions we've learned and try them out in other keys we've worked with as well.

We'll finish this chapter by trying out some walking bass lines in "Sammy Snake"—the song we learned back in Chapter 7. We'll add a walking bass line in measure 2, moving from the Am to the D chord, and then put another in to walk back to Am (measure 4). Then we'll also add one in measure 6, moving between the D and G chords. (And we'll repeat all of these runs in the second half of the verse.) In the chorus, we'll add just one run moving between D and Am in measure 20. Notice how here we go all the way down to the open E string and walk up to the Am chord, instead of walking down to the Am, as we did in measure 4. We've got a longer break here, and this longer run acts as a nice fill in its place.

SAMMY SNAKE

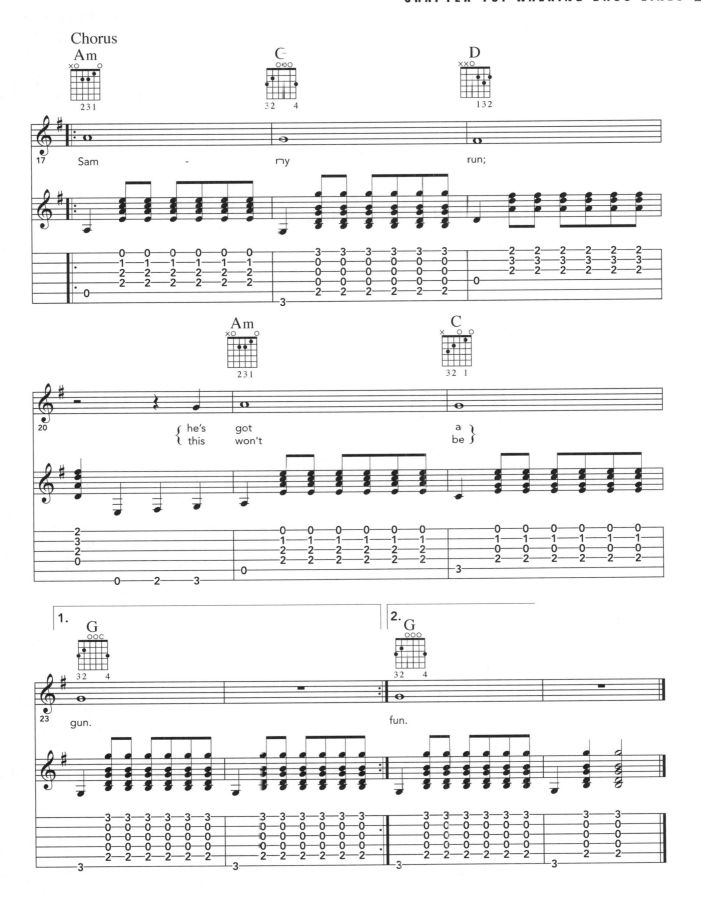

CHAPTER 16: MORE MINOR KEY PROGRESSIONS

In this chapter, we'll learn a few more minor key progressions. We'll start with the i–♭VII–♭VI, a staple of the classic rock realm, and we'll also explore the minor blues.

The i–♭VII–♭VI Progression

We've already worked with the ♭VII chord, and we know that we can find that chord if we walk down (or backwards) one whole step (or two frets on the guitar) from the I chord in a major key. The same holds true for our ♭VII chord in a minor key, when we're walking back from a minor i chord. In fact, it holds even *more* true in minor keys. That's because the ♭VII chord *comes* from minor keys, and we just "borrowed" it in our major key progressions. So when you walk up (or down) the minor scale to find your chords, you'll get a ♭VII chord at the seventh degree and a ♭VI chord at the sixth degree. Let's try this out in the key of Em. Since we're in the key of Em, that's our i chord. Walking back down the E minor scale gives us the following (hint: there's only one sharp in E minor—F♯): E (1), D (7), C (6). So our ♭VII chord is D, and our ♭VI chord is C, making our i–♭VII–♭VI progression Em–D–C. Here's how that sounds:

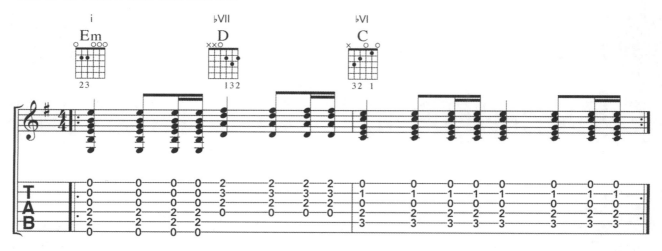

You'll recognize this progression from many classic rock tunes, such as "All Along the Watchtower." This sounds great as it is, but another nice variation moves back through the ♭VII (D) chord on the way back to the i (Em) chord. If you play it this way, it sounds more like the ending to songs like "Stairway to Heaven."

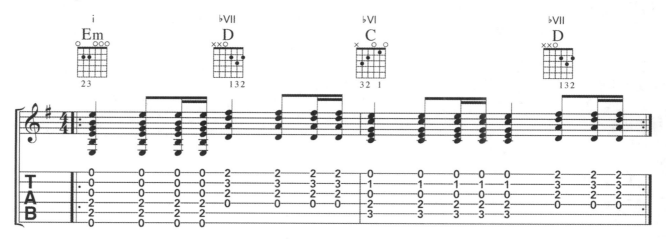

TIP: WHY DO I COUNT BACKWARDS FROM 1 AND GET 7?

Since there are only seven notes, there are only seven degrees in a scale. This means that, when you go up the scale from the first degree, after you reach 7, the next note is the same as 1—only an *octave* higher (an octave is the distance between two notes of the same letter name). So when we count *backwards* from 1, it makes sense that the next note would be 7. We could easily count *up* the scale to find our sixth and seventh degrees, but it's just a little quicker to find those scale degrees by counting backwards, and that's why we're doing that here.

Let's try our new progression out in the key of Am. If we're in the key of Am, then that's the i chord, so let's count down from A to find the other two (*hint: the key of Am has no sharps or flats*): A (1), G (7), F (6). So G is our ♭VII chord and F is our ♭VI chord, making our i–♭VII–♭VI progression Am–G–F:

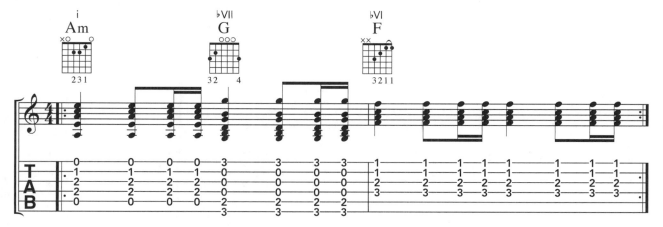

Let's try our variation out now in this key—where we move back through the ♭VII chord (G) to get to Am:

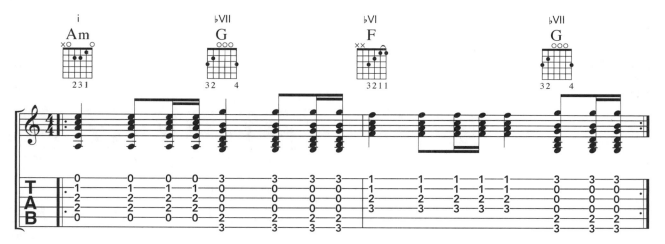

The Minor Blues

A basic minor blues progression uses the same pattern as a major blues, except that it uses all minor chords. Translating that to a minor progression would mean you'd have this as your chord map:

i				
iv		i		
v	iv	i		

Applying this to the key of Am, our basic minor blues would look like this:

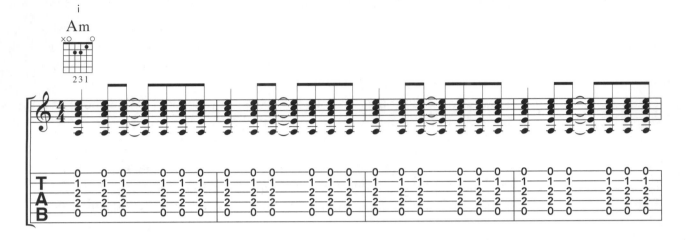

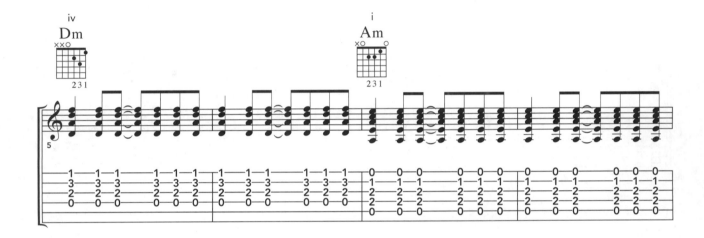

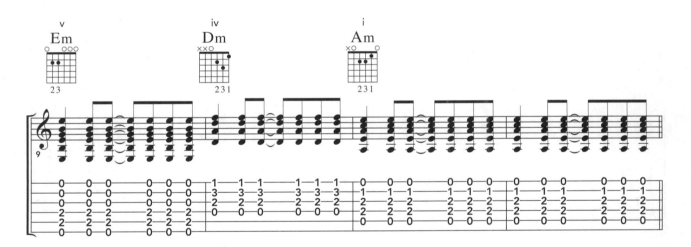

We can also add a "quick iv" to our minor blues, just as we did with the major blues. This means we'll go up to the iv chord in measure 2 and move quickly back to the i chord in measure 3, like this:

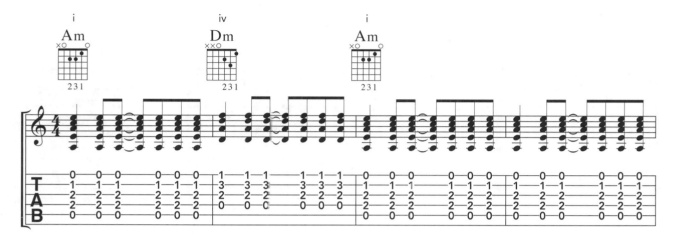

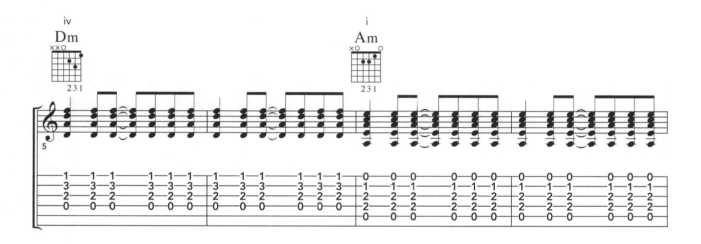

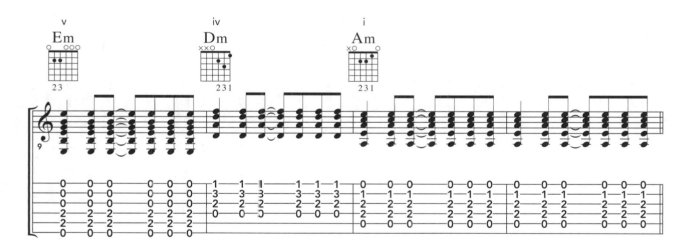

For our final touch, let's add a turnaround. Similar to what we did in the major blues, here we'll go to the minor v chord in the last measure (instead of the major V).

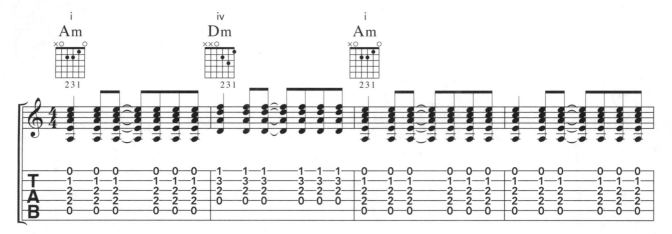

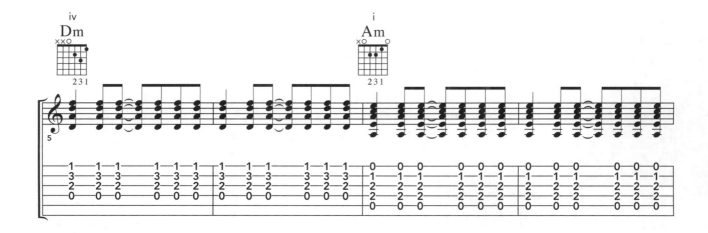

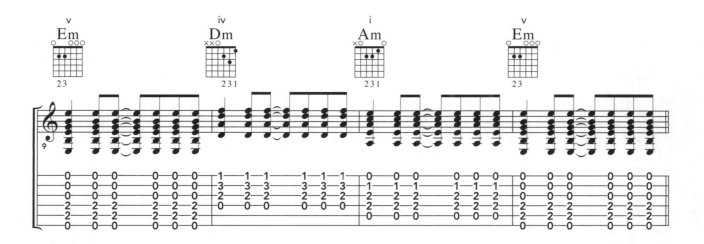

Minor Blues with Dominant IV and V Chords

There are tons of ways people play the minor blues, and it often gets so jazzed up it's hard to recognize what's what! But one of the more common moves is to use dominant IV or V chords in place of their minor chord counterparts. Let's try this out with our minor blues in Am. We'll start off by seeing how it sounds if we only use a dominant V chord (E7):

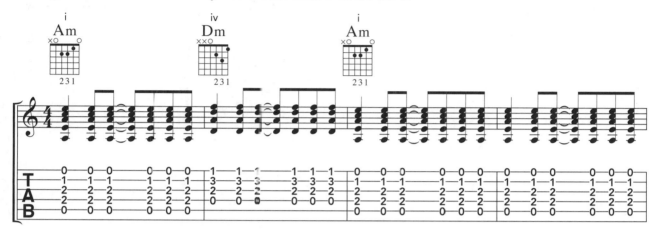

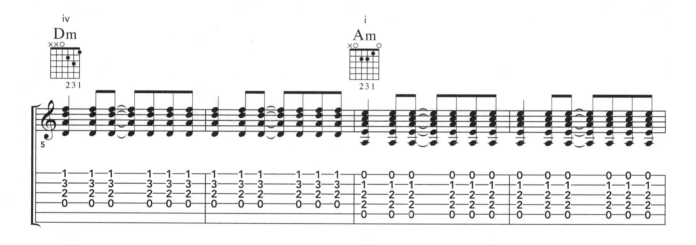

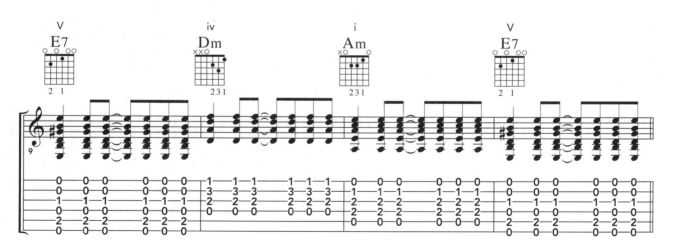

Now let's try out our minor blues using dominant IV chords as well as dominant V chords throughout:

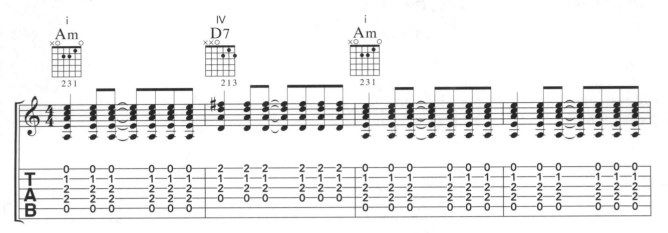

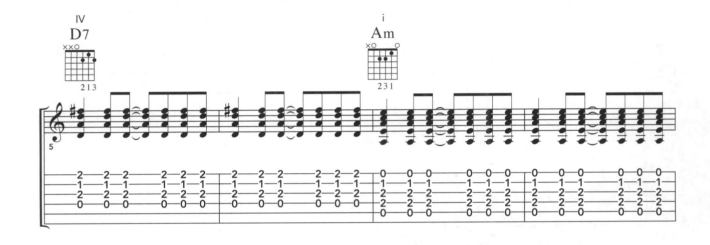

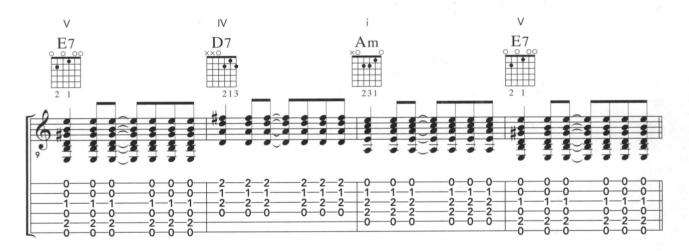

As you can see, there are plenty of ways to make our minor blues sound a little different. Now you already have at least four or five ways of playing this blues progression!

Let's finish off with a blues song, "Minor Chord Blues." This tune is similar to the "Dominant Seventh Blues" from previous chapters, but is played in a minor key. Here, we'll play minor chords for the i (Em) and iv (Am) chords, but we'll use dominant chords for the V (B7). On the video, I'll use the same strum pattern as the previous example, but you feel free to try out your own strum patterns and variations.

MINOR CHORD BLUES

SECTION III:
Fingerpicking

CHAPTER 17: GETTING STARTED WITH FINGERPICKING

Fingerpicking our guitars gives us a whole new set of sounds and musical styles that we can play—from singer/songwriter fingerpicking accompaniment to the many regions of blues fingerpicking to advanced fingerstyle or classical playing. We already know about using our fretting hand (for right-handed players, that's your left hand), so the first thing we'll need to learn about is our picking hand.

The Picking Hand

When fingerpicking, you use your picking-hand fingers instead of a pick to play the strings on your guitar. Right-handed players use their right hand, while left-handed players use their left hand. Here is a picture of the picking hand on the guitar strings.

Some fingerpickers use just their thumb and index finger to pick, while others use up to all five fingers. We'll work on using the most common set of fingers: your thumb and three fingers (everything except the pinky). In the music, the fingers on your picking hand are often referred to in this way:

p = thumb

i = index

m = middle

a = ring

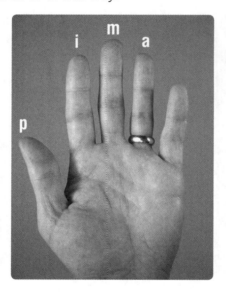

TIP: WHY IS MY THUMB CALLED THE "P" FINGER?

You've probably noticed that the fingering letters don't all match the first letter of each finger. That's because these letters come from the Spanish words for each of those fingers (pulgar, indice, medio, and anular).

Here is how these pick-hand fingerings look in the context of a musical passage. Note how the fingerings are positioned between the music notation and tablature:

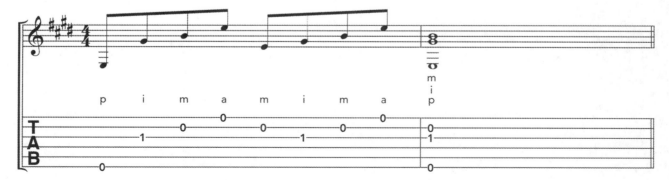

To help highlight and separate the thumb from the fingers, music notation often splits the parts by showing notes played by the thumb with stems pointing down and notes played with the fingers with stems pointing up:

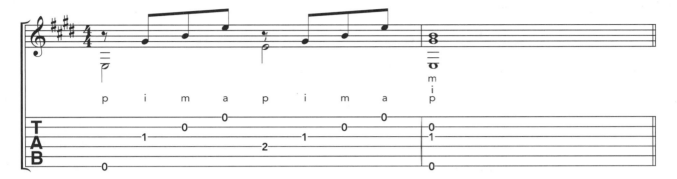

FINGERPICKS VS. BARE FINGERS

Many players fingerpick with their bare fingers, and some grow their nails out to provide a brighter attack when plucking the strings. If your nails break easily, but you prefer the brighter sound of nails, you can have them fortified at a nail salon. Some pickers use plastic or metal fingerpicks for their thumb and fingers to help create a bright sound. It's easiest to start with your bare fingers (or nails), but experiment with other methods to find the sound and feel that you prefer. All of the examples in the video portion of this book were played with bare fingers and medium-length nails to provide a brighter attack.

First Fingerpicking Pattern

Let's start by simply plucking the low E string with our thumb. We'll use what's called a "free stroke" here, which means that, after you pluck the note, your thumb will move up and away from the strings, instead of resting on the next string below. Let's start slowly by playing one bass note in the measure (one note every four beats), repeating that measure as we get comfortable plucking the string:

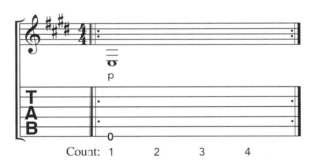

TIP: FREE STROKE VS. REST STROKE

Classical guitarists use two types of strokes: the *free stroke* and the *rest stroke*. For a rest stroke, your thumb (or finger) will pluck a string and then come to rest on the next string. For a free stroke, your thumb (or finger) plucks the string and then stays "free" by generally moving up and away from the guitar. Folk and blues fingerpickers most commonly use free strokes, and that's what we'll focus on in this and the upcoming chapters. For a thorough discussion on free strokes and rest strokes (as well as a comprehensive method on beginning through advanced fingerstyle playing), see the *Alex de Grassi Guitar Method* (String Letter Publishing).

Now try playing a bass note on *every* beat, like this:

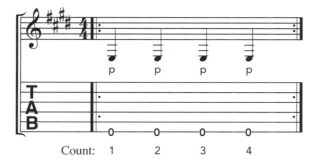

Now let's fret an E7 chord and begin to incorporate our fingers. We'll play the third string with our i finger and start by repeating one note in a measure, like this:

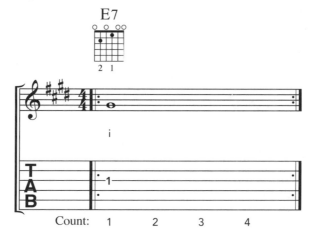

Next, let's try plucking that third string with our index finger on *every* beat:

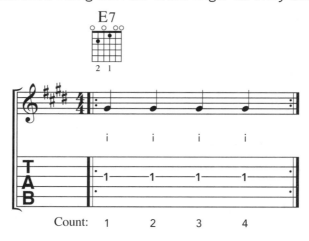

Now let's put our thumb and index fingers together by alternating between them. We'll play a thumb stroke on beats 1 and 3 and an index-finger pluck on beats 2 and 4:

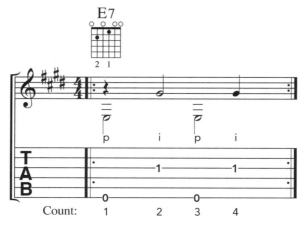

You're already playing a fingerpicking pattern! You can use this pattern for any six-string chord. For any five-string chord, all you have to do is move your thumb up to the fifth string. Let's try this with an A7 chord. Remember that while your thumb moves up a string, your index finger *stays* in the same place:

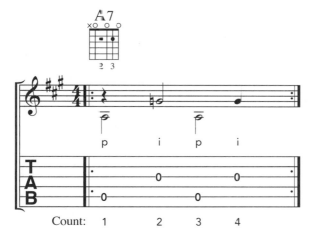

For a four-string chord, all you have to do is move your thumb up to the fourth string (again, leaving your index finger on the third string). Let's try this out with a D7 chord:

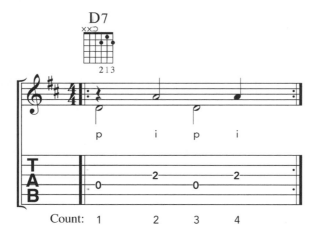

Now that we can play many different chords with this pattern, let's try it out with a ii–V–I progression in D:

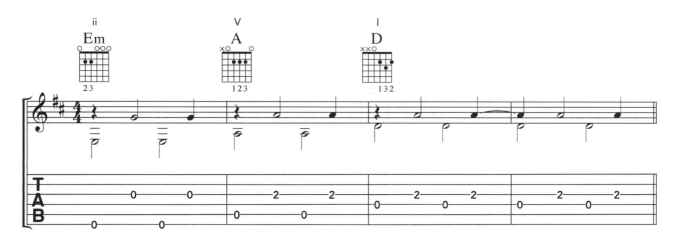

For a little more fun, let's use this pattern in a full blues in E, using dominant seventh chords throughout:

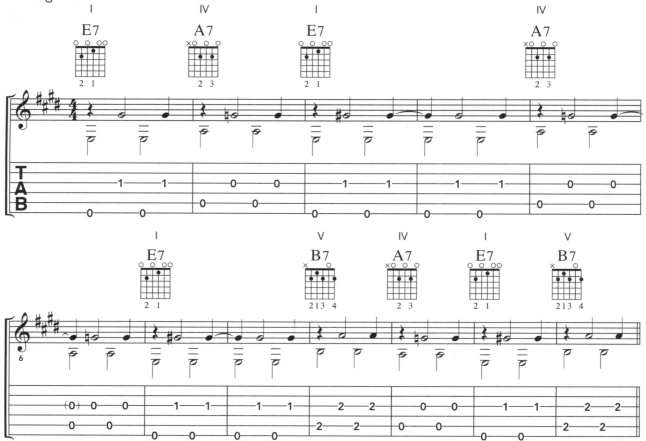

Adding Your Middle Finger

We'll use our middle finger to pluck the second string. Let's start by plucking that string once a measure while we fret an E7 chord:

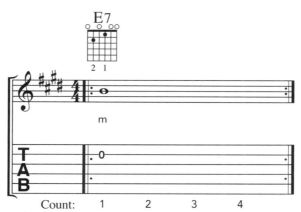

Now let's try plucking that string every beat:

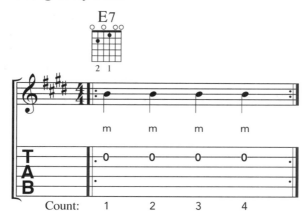

Now let's try alternating between the thumb and middle finger on our E7 chord:

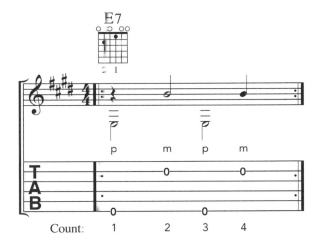

Next, let's try this pattern with a i–bVII–bVI chord progression in Am (Am–G–F). Remember that your thumb will move to the string that has the bass notes (the lowest notes) of each chord, while your middle finger stays on the second string the whole time:

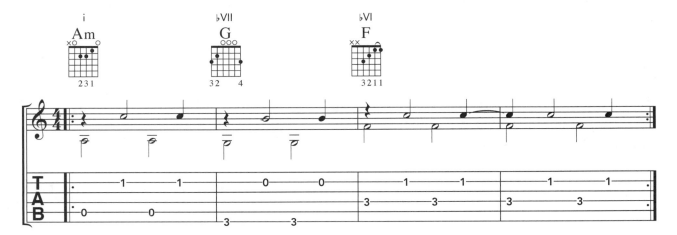

Middle and Index Finger Together

You can add a little punch to your sound by playing two fingers together. Let's try plucking our index and middle fingers together over an E7 chord:

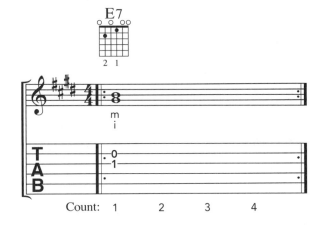

Now let's try this on *every* beat:

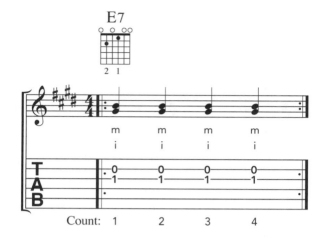

Next, let's try alternating these with bass notes, like this:

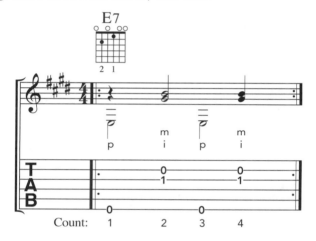

When we add this pattern into our E blues, we can see how much one finger really fills things out:

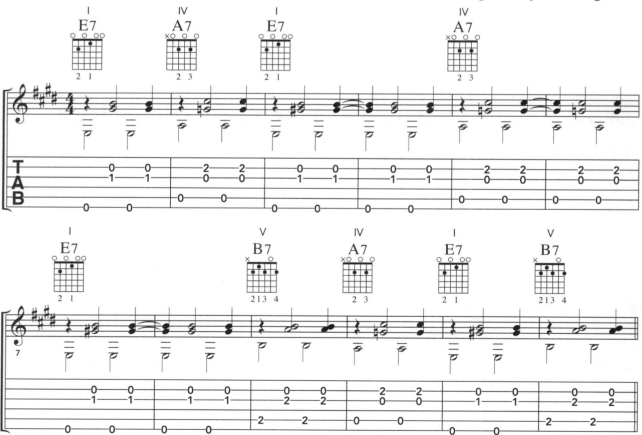

Adding the Ring Finger

Now let's try using our ring finger. We'll use it on the first string, like this, and we'll try plucking a note on every beat:

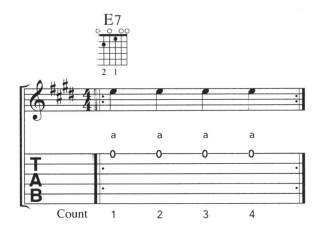

Now let's alternate that ring finger with the thumb:

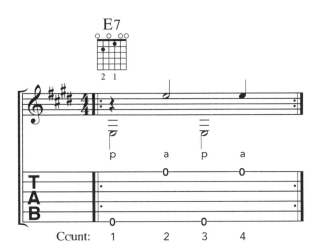

Let's try this pattern out with a I–vi–ii–V progression in C (C–Am–Dm–G). Just like with the other patterns, our thumb will move to the lowest string of each chord, while our ring finger stays on the first string:

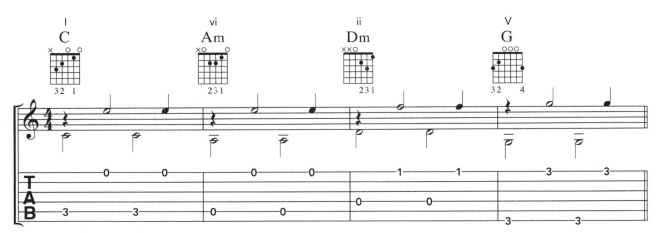

Three Fingers Together

Now let's try plucking our index, middle, and ring fingers all together! We'll play them every beat, but slow it down to once per measure first if you're having trouble.

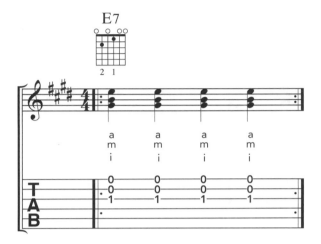

Let's work this into a pattern by alternating with our thumb:

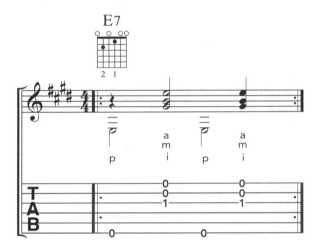

And now for our grand finale! Let's try this pattern out with our E blues tune, the "Dominant Seventh Blues" (which we learned in Chapter 11). Here, every chord is even a little thicker than it was when we plucked two strings together. Pluck the final note with your thumb.

DOMINANT SEVENTH BLUES

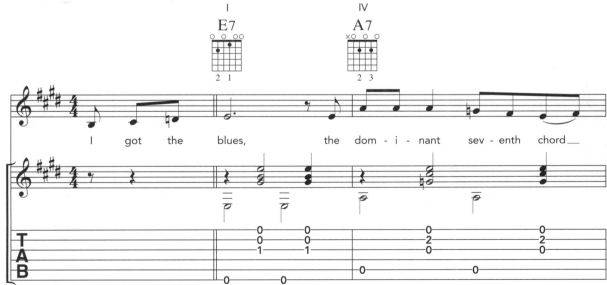

CHAPTER 18: ROLLING FINGERPICKING

You can use several fingers in a row to create rolling patterns that work well with a variety of different time signatures. In this lesson, we'll look at several different ways to work all of our fingers into patterns to accompany ourselves on songs.

Thumb–Index–Middle (p i m) Pattern

The first pattern we'll look at uses our thumb and index finger, as we did in the previous chapter, but then adds a middle finger pluck after the index finger. We'll try this pattern out in 3/4 time, which has three beats in each measure (*for more on 3/4 time, see the nearby sidebar*). Count along ("1, 2, 3…1, 2, 3…") as you play this example so that you can get comfortable with the feel of 3/4 time.

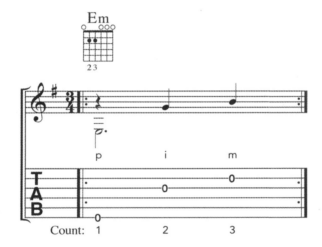

As you can see, this pattern works great in 3/4 time, since you play a note with a different finger on each beat.

3/4 TIME

In Chapter 14, we learned that the top note in a time signature tells us how many beats per measure we'll have. So, in 3/4 time, we have three beats per measure. We also learned that if we take the bottom number and consider it a fraction under the number "1," we'll know what note duration gets a beat. When we do this for 3/4 time, we get 1/4—meaning a quarter note gets a beat. Putting that together, 3/4 time has three beats in a measure, and a quarter note gets a beat.

Let's try this pattern out on a i–♭VII–♭VI progression in Em (Em–D–C). Remember that your thumb will move to whichever string is the lowest note of the chord. So for the Em chord, play the sixth string, for the D chord, play the fourth string, and for the C chord, play the fifth string.

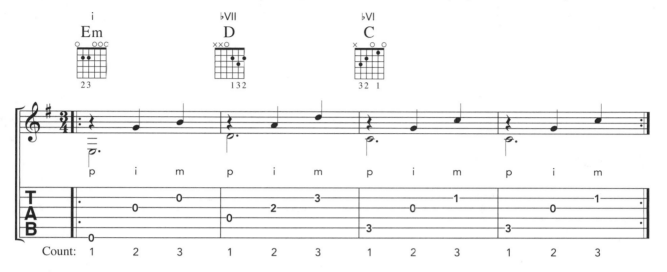

Let's try this out with one more progression: a I–IV–V progression in A (A–D–E):

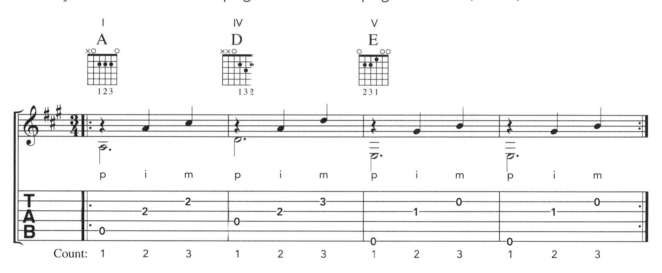

This pattern works great in 3/4 time, but what happens when we want to play something in 4/4 time? We only have three notes, so we can't fill out the measure, but if we add another index finger pluck at the end, we now have four beats:

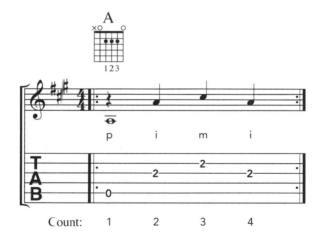

This creates an up-and-down rolling pattern that works well in any chord progression in 4/4 time. Next, let's try a ii–V–I progression in the key of C (Dm–G–C).

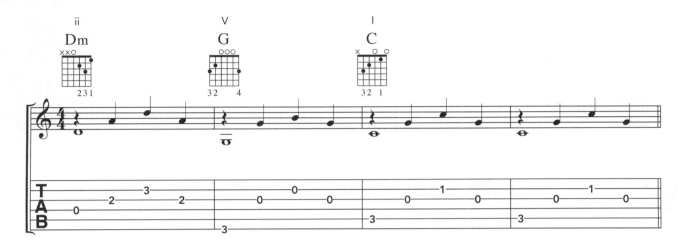

Adding the Ring Finger (p i m a)

We get another great pattern for 4/4 time when we add our ring finger to the basic p-i-m pattern we started with. Let's try that using a C chord:

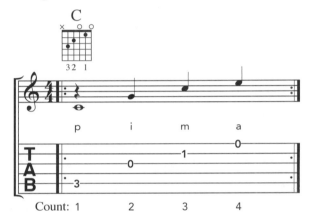

Let's try this out with a full 12-bar blues progression in the key of G using dominant seventh chords:

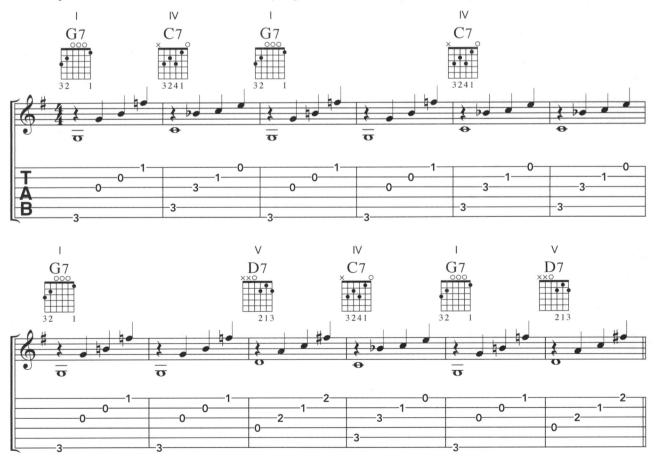

So now we have several patterns and can play in 3/4 and 4/4 time. If we add one more note to our newest pattern, we can play in 6/8 time, too! (*We looked at 6/8 time in Chapter 14; there are six beats, and each eighth note gets a beat.*) This new pattern rolls back through the middle and index finger at the end, creating a rolling six-note pattern like this:

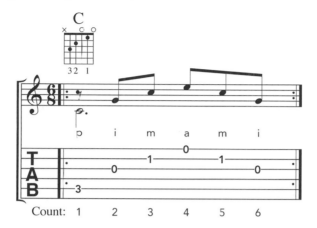

There's a lot going on here, so don't worry if this takes a while to get under your fingers! Remember to work with a metronome and slow things down to a pace at which you can play it, then gradually work it up to speed. You may recognize this as a common pattern in songs like REM's "Everybody Hurts."

Now let's try our rolling pattern with a I–vi–ii–V progression in the key of C (C–Am–Dm–G):

It sounds so good with the I–vi–ii–V progression, let's try it in another key—G (G–Em–Am–D):

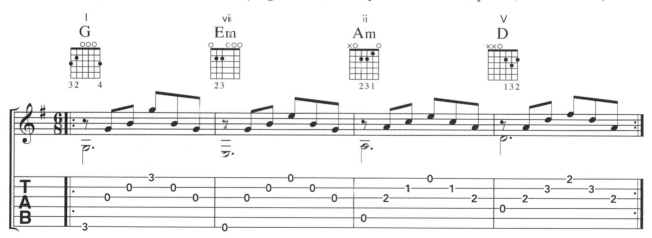

Let's finish the chapter by playing a song with one of our new patterns. We'll use the p-i-m-a pattern to play "Saving My Kisses," which we played with several different strumming patterns earlier in the book. Our p-i-m-a fingerpicking pattern turns the song from an upbeat rocker into a bit of a ballad:

SAVING MY KISSES

CHAPTER 19: PINCHES

In Chapter 17, we plucked two or more strings with our fingers at the same time. With a *pinch*, we pluck with a finger *and* our thumb at the same time. Adding pinches to your playing can help you create new fingerpicking patterns and vary your old ones. Later on, when you begin playing intermediate and advanced fingerpicking, pinches can help you add melody notes on top of your fingerpicking patterns.

Pinching with the Index Finger

Let's start by pinching a note with our thumb and index finger, like this:

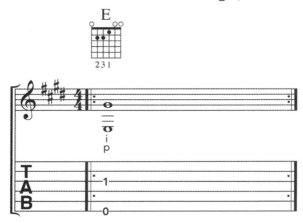

Now we'll speed that up so our finger gets comfortable and ready to play it in the flow of a musical passage:

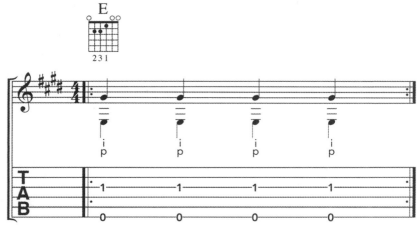

Next, let's work the pinch into a fingerpicking pattern. We'll start with our pinch, then follow that with our middle finger and ring finger. This pattern works well in 3/4 time:

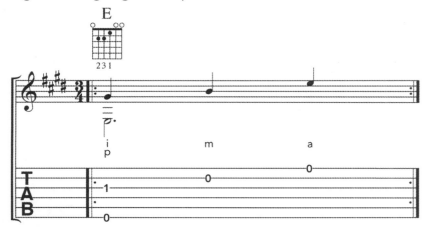

Practice this pattern with your chord progressions. Here's a i–♭VII–♭VI in the key of Em to get you started (Em–D–C):

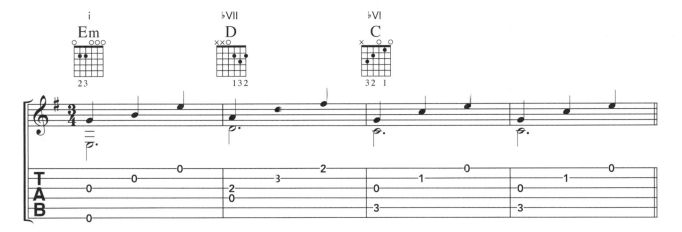

Of course, since we often play in 4/4 time, it's nice to have a pattern that works in that time signature, too. If we add our middle finger in at the end of the pattern, this creates a rolling pattern that moves back to our index finger pinch. and it works well in 4/4 time:

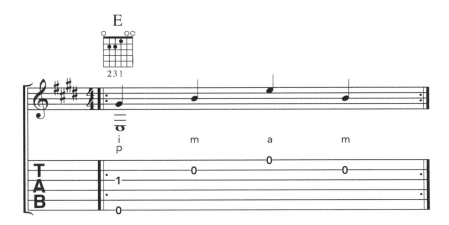

Let's take this pattern for a drive with our I–♭VII–IV progression in the key of E (E–D–A):

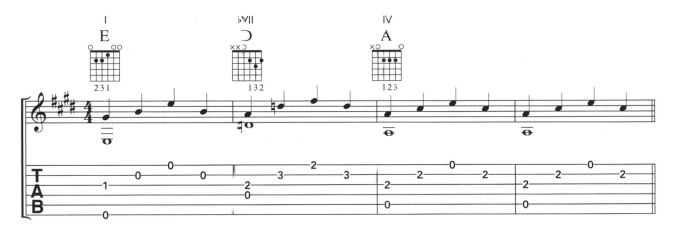

Pinching with the Middle Finger

Now let's try pinching with the middle finger. Start off slowly, with one pinch per measure, and then pinch four times a measure until you're comfortable with this motion:

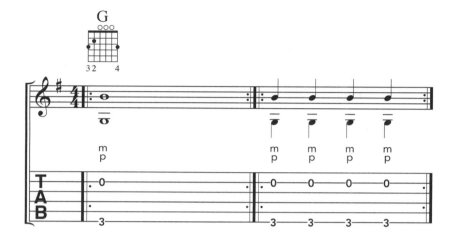

We can play this pinch in patterns that work in 3/4 time, but it's not quite as straightforward as our index finger pinch pattern. Let's try the pinch, then follow that with the ring finger and index finger. This creates a naturally rolling pattern in 3/4 time:

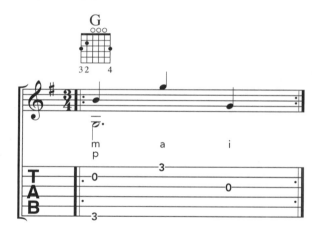

Now try that out in some chord progressions. Here's a I–vi–ii–V in the key of G to get you started (G–Em–Am–D):

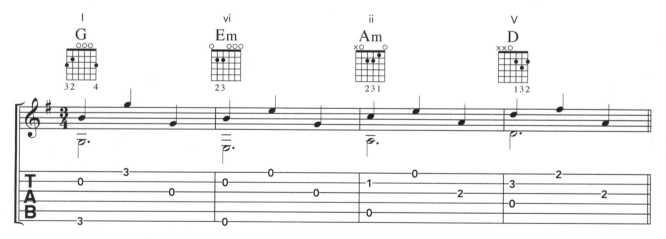

You could also *reverse* this rolling pattern by starting with the pinch, then plucking with your index finger, and finishing with your ring finger Here's how that would sound:

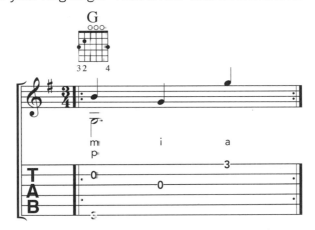

Let's see how that sounds with our I–vi–ii–V progression in G:

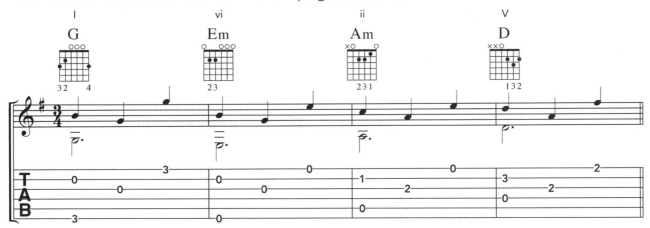

Now let's try a pattern that works in 4/4 time. We'll start with our middle finger pinch, then pluck with our index, middle, and ring fingers to create a down-and-up pattern like this:

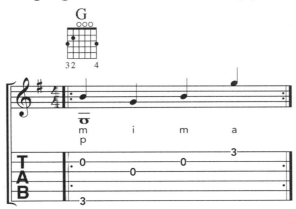

Let's take this pattern for a spin on our I–IV–V progression in G (G–C–D)

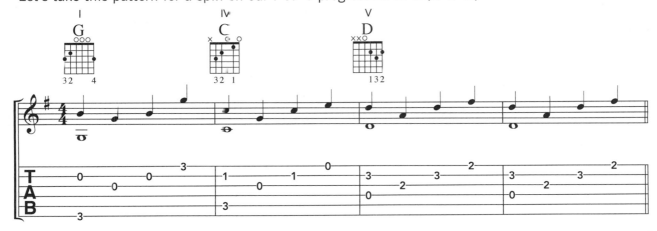

We could also reverse this pattern by starting with the pinch, then plucking with our ring, middle, and index fingers, in that order:

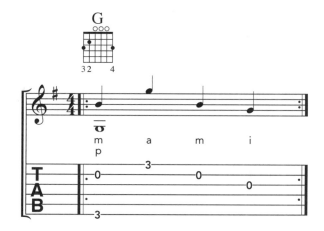

Let's see how this variation sounds with our I–IV–V progression in G:

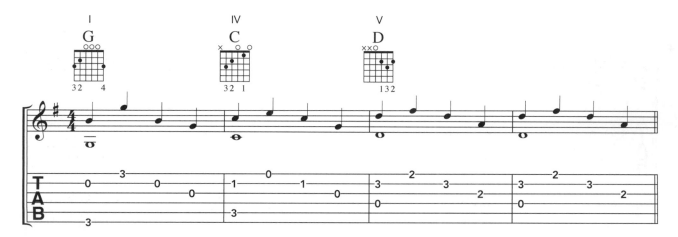

Pinching with the Ring Finger

Now that we can pinch with our index and middle fingers, let's practice pinching with our ring finger as well. Start slowly, then work your pinches up to speed:

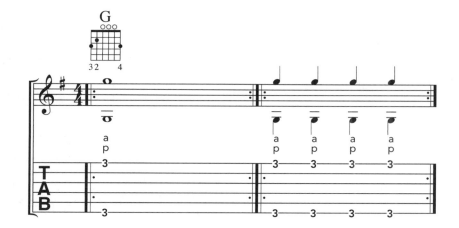

Our ring finger pinch works perfectly in 3/4 time if we follow it up with the middle finger, then the index, like this:

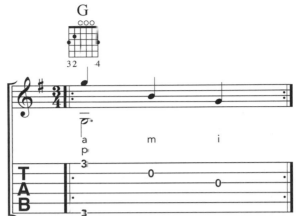

Let's try this pattern with a I–♭VII–IV progression in the key of G (G–F–C):

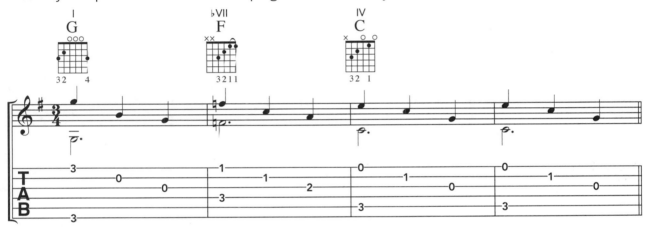

To play in 4/4 time, you can add a middle finger pluck to the end, creating this rolling pattern:

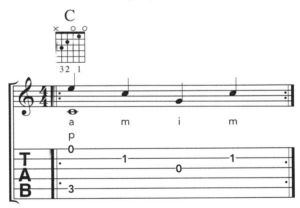

Try this out with a few chord progressions. Here it is in a I–vi–ii–V progression in C (C–Am–Dm–G) to get you started:

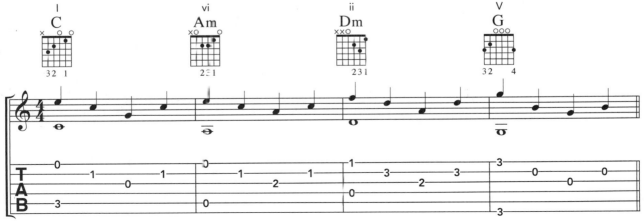

Mixing Pinches and Patterns

We can mix up our patterns and pinches to create even more patterns. For instance, we could take our rolling 4/4 pattern from Chapter 18 and add it to one of our middle finger pinch patterns to get this extended pattern:

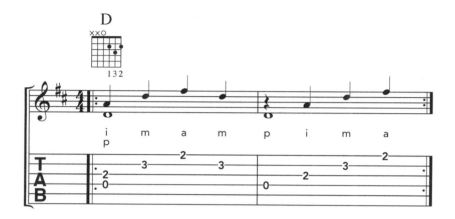

Try this out with a I–♭VII–IV progression in D (D–C–G). You could play it so that you cycle all the way through the pattern for each chord change (playing the pattern twice for the G chord):

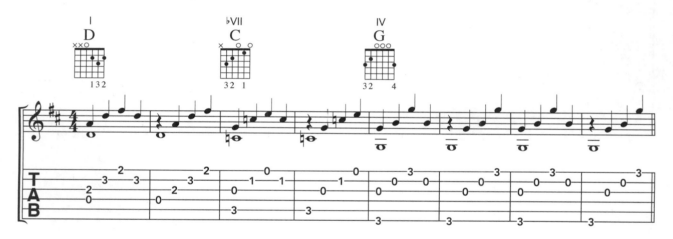

Or, you could change chords more quickly. This means you'd change from the D to the C chord in the middle of the pattern:

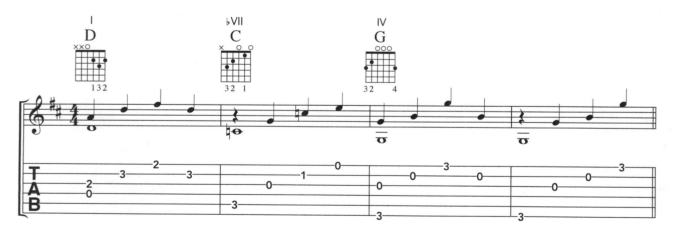

TIP: VARY YOUR CHORD CHANGES

The chord progressions we've learned in this book are often put together in common ways. But you can always vary the length of any chord in the progression to change the sound. Give it a try! You'll generally find that your progressions sound better when they fill out an even number of measures (like four or eight), but you can always experiment with *when* you change the chords to discover new progressions and inspire new sounds.

You could also play more than one pinch in a pattern. However, too many pinches can make your flowing patterns sound clunky and hard to play! For instance, this pattern that pinches with all three fingers in a row isn't something you'd use that often:

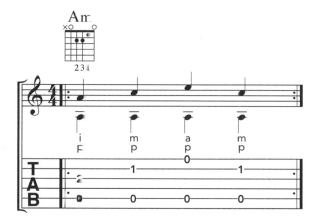

You can also mix your fingers and pinches up in completely new ways. Here's a pattern that starts with your thumb, index, middle, and index in a row (p i m i), then goes to a pinch with the ring finger, followed by the index, middle, and index again:

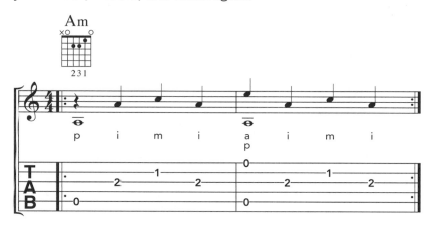

Let's try this pattern out on a i–♭VII–♭VI progression in the key of Am (Am–G–F):

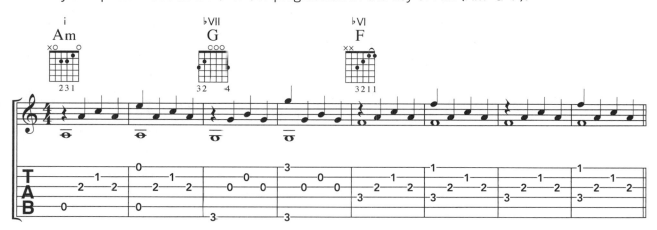

We've played all these examples as quarter-note patterns, but you often see patterns like this played with eighth notes. When you're really comfortable with all these patterns, you can speed them up to eighth-note subdivisions. Let's try that out with our last picking pattern:

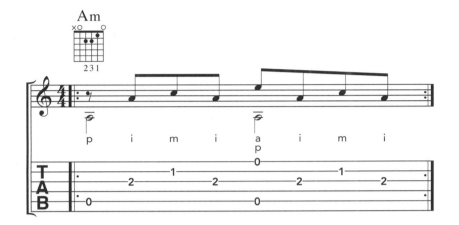

Let's practice this final pattern in a song. We'll use "Home to Alaska," which we learned back in Chapter 14. Check out how our fingerpicking pattern gives the song a completely different feel; while the strummed version would be great for a noisy jam, this version works great as a solo piece in a quiet setting.

Watch out for the chord change from E to D, which happens in the middle of our pattern. If you have problems with that section (or any other), isolate the measure and slow it down (without the vocals). Once you're comfortable enough playing the pattern over the chords without thinking about it, you're ready to add the vocals back in.

For the last chord, pluck with your thumb, index, middle, and ring fingers all at the same time.

HOME TO ALASKA

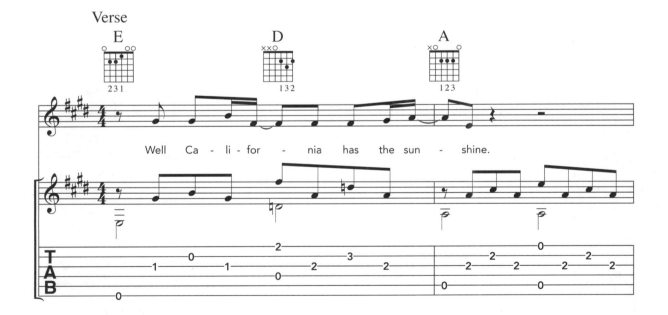

If you mess with Tex - as, you're a fool. ___   But no state's big-ger than A-las-

- ka.   I miss my home, and that's ___ the truth. ___

Chorus

I'm head-ing home to A-las-ka ___   to see those moun-tains and the

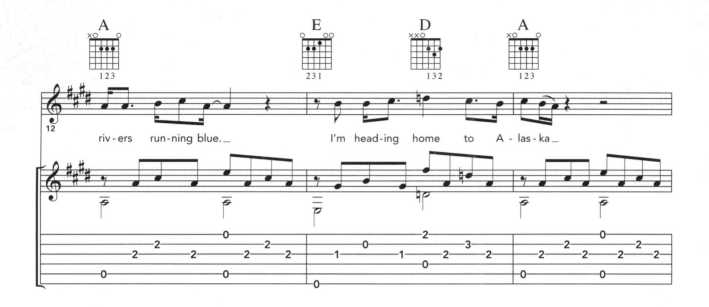

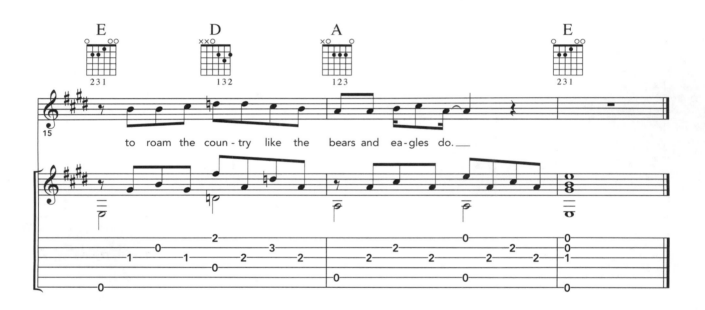

CHAPTER 20: THE ALTERNATING BASS

When we were playing with a pick, we learned how to play bass notes on alternate strings in Chapter 9 (Alternate-Bass Strumming). We can do the same thing with our fingers. Commonly called *alternate-bass fingerpicking*, this technique helps us fill out the sound of our fingerpicking patterns even more.

Picking Six-String Chords

To play six-string chords like E, we'll start with the low sixth string as our first bass note. So far, our thumb has only been playing once or twice each measure, but alternate-bass fingerpicking requires us to play on *every* beat—four times a measure! To get comfortable with this, let's start by playing the open sixth string four times each measure:

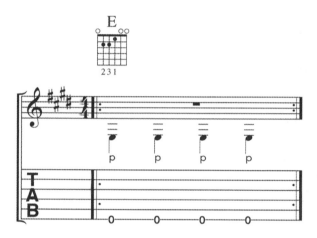

Now, let's alternate that bass note between the sixth and fourth strings while holding down an E chord shape:

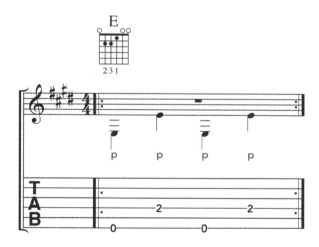

This is our thumb pattern for all six-string chords. Next, let's start adding in the fingers. We'll start by using our middle finger to play the second string on the "and" of beat 1—the eighth note between beats 1 and 2.

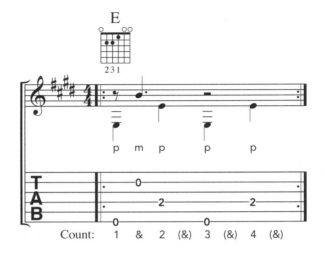

Make sure to count along and slow things down if you have trouble working this finger in. Once you're comfortable with this pattern, add your index finger into the mix. Use it to play the third string on the "and" of beat 2.

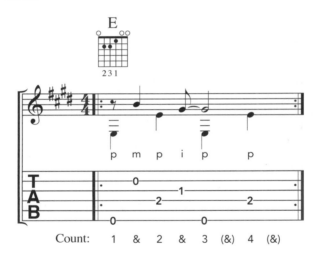

You're almost there! Now, all we need to do is repeat the pattern from the first half of the measure. This means your middle finger plucks the second string again on the "and" of beat 3, and your index finger plucks the third string again on the "and" of beat 4:

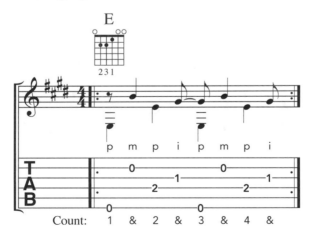

There you have it! You're now playing alternate-bass fingerpicking. This pattern works for any six-string chord, like G, for instance:

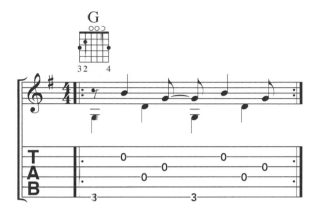

Picking Five-String Chords

To pick five-string chords, all we have to do is shift our thumb up to play the bass note on the fifth string for beats 1 and 3. It continues to play notes on the fourth string on beats 2 and 4. Let's try this out while holding down an A chord shape:

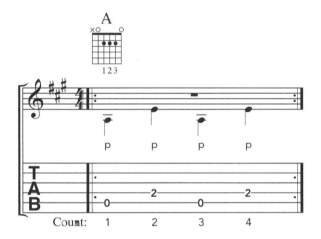

Next, let's add in the fingers. They'll play the same strings that they did for the six-string pattern—the second and third strings:

This pattern works for any five-string chord, like C, for instance:

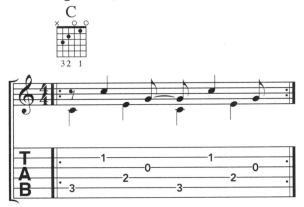

Let's practice moving between a six-string chord and a five-string chord so our thumb gets comfortable moving between the patterns. Here's a G–C progression:

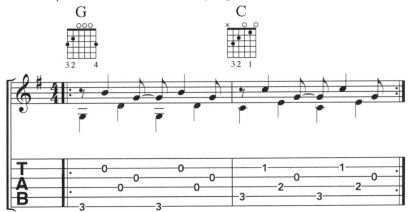

Also try it out on an E–A progression, like this:

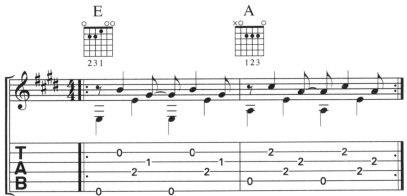

Picking Four-String Chords

To pick four-string chords, we need to shift our thumb *up* a string set from our five-string pattern. This means that, instead of picking the fifth and fourth strings, here we'll alternate between the fourth and third strings. Let's try this out while holding down a D chord:

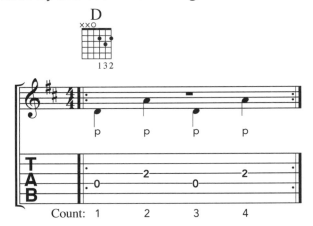

For four-string chords, we'll need to shift our fingers up a string set as well. This means that our index finger moves up to the second string, while our middle finger moves up to the first string. Let's add these fingers into the pattern over a D chord:

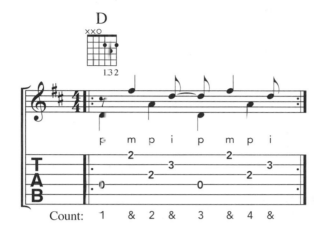

Now that you have the six-, five-, and four-string patterns down, let's practice them together so that your thumb gets comfortable moving from position to position. A I–IV–V progression in the key of G (G–C–D) is a great way to practice this, since it moves between all three patterns:

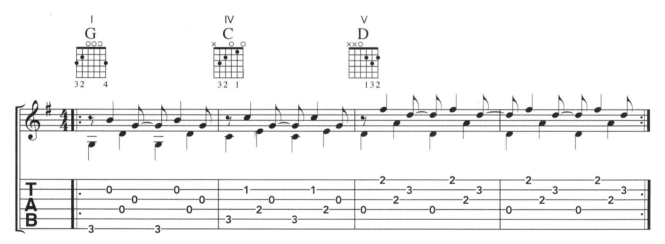

Remember to move those fingers up a string set when you get to the D chord! Another good progression to test out these patterns is a –♭VII–IV progression in the key of E (E–D–A):

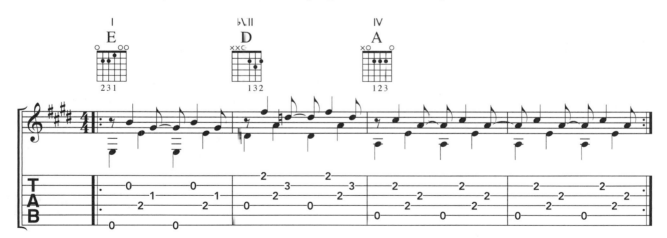

TIP: PLUCK OPEN STRINGS WHILE CHANGING CHORDS

When you play picking patterns like this, it can be near impossible to change your chords between the last eighth note of one measure and the downbeat of the next measure. The trick is that you don't have to do this! You can start changing your chord on the last eighth note of a measure (or the last full beat, even). While your fret-hand fingers are moving into place for the next chord shape, your picking hand will pick the open strings. This may sound funny at a slow speed, but within the context of a song or progression, it actually sounds fine, and *everybody* does it! Here's how that I–bVII–IV progression in E sounds when we do this:

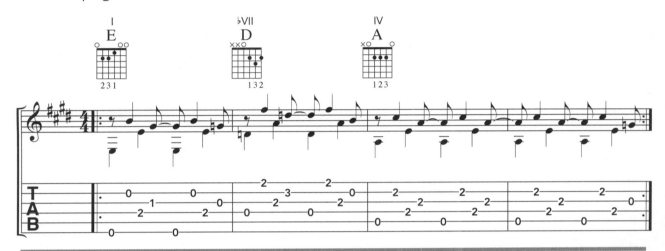

Let's finish things off by putting our alternate-bass fingerpicking pattern to use in a song. We played "Sammy Snake" earlier in the book with alternate-bass strums and walking bass lines. Here, the song gets a different sound backed up with our alternate-bass fingerpicking. The picking pattern holds steady throughout the song until the final measure, where you pluck four strings with all your fingers and thumb at the same time. Try rolling this chord by playing the notes quickly in order from low to high with your thumb, index, middle, and ring fingers.

SAMMY SNAKE

Verse

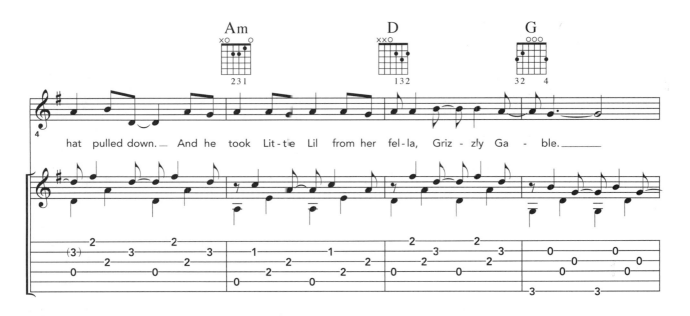

hat pulled down.— And he took Lit-tle Lil from her fel-la, Griz-zly Ga - ble._____

But Sam-my Snake nev-er real-ly had a chance.—

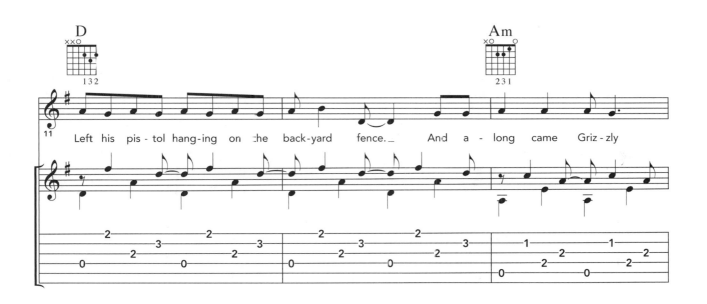

Left his pis-tol hang-ing on the back-yard fence.— And a-long came Griz-zly

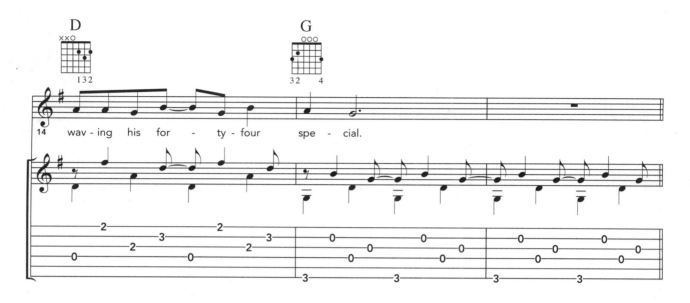

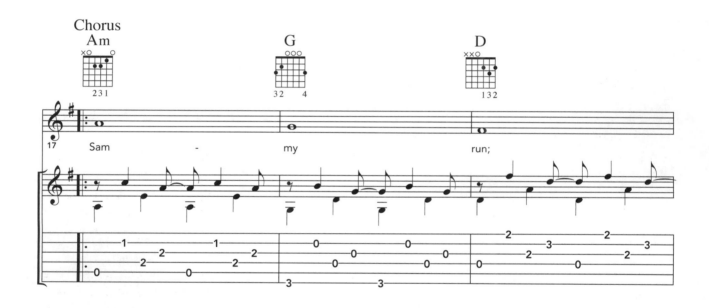

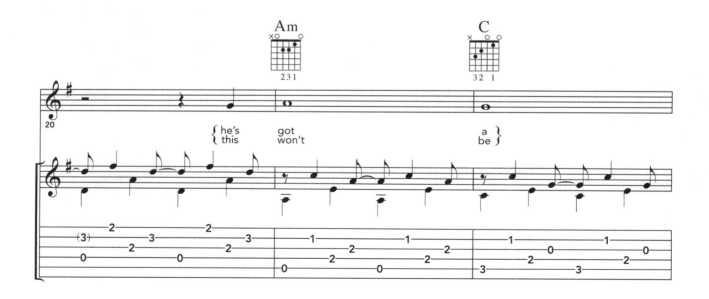

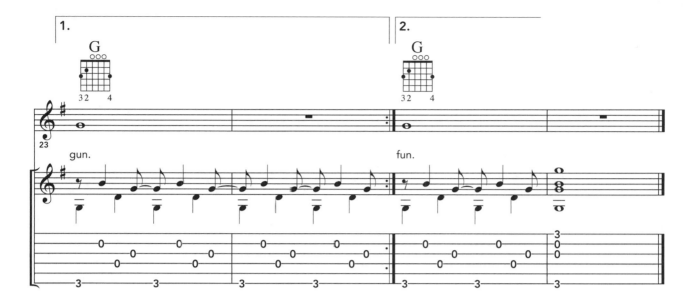

Congratulations!

You can now strum, play chord changes, and fingerpick your guitar. So give yourself a pat on the back and go out and play some songs with your friends!

Now that you're ready to move on, there are many great books out there to help you continue learning. If you want to continue mostly as a fingerpicker, *Travis Picking* (Hal Leonard) by Andrew DuBrock can teach you how to vary these alternate-bass fingerpicking patterns even more in your songs. You'll also learn how to use these patterns to pick solo tunes like your acoustic blues heroes and more advanced patterns like Nashville greats Merle Travis and Chet Atkins did.

If you'd like to increase all your skills—your fingerpicking and strumming as well as learning to play lead guitar and melodies—*Total Acoustic Guitar* (also by Andrew DuBrock) will help you get there. This book teaches a variety of strumming and picking techniques—like scratch rhythm, power chords, and open-string chords—to help you accompany yourself with a pick like modern acoustic rock, blues, and folk players. It also expands your fingerpicking techniques to shine light on playing melodies over monotonic bass fingerpicking and takes a step into modern fingerstyle guitar. Lead sections include instruction on pentatonic, blues, and major and minor scales and how to create melodies and solos from each one of these. For more information on either of these books, please visit **www.andrewdubrock.com**.

APPENDIX

Chords

Here are all the chords we've learned in this book:

MAJOR CHORDS

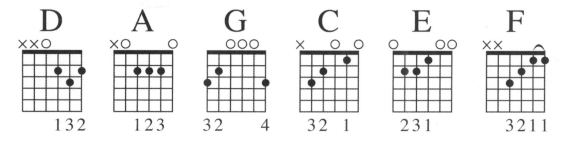

D   A   G   C   E   F

MINOR CHORDS

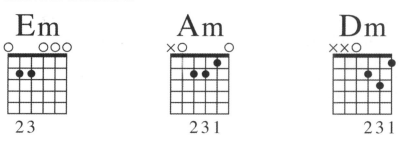

Em   Am   Dm

DOMINANT SEVENTH CHORDS

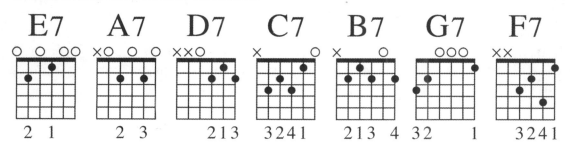

E7 A7 D7 C7 B7 G7 F7

Reading Music

In music notation, horizontal lines and the spaces in between are used to represent notes. There are five horizontal lines in each grouping, and the group is called a *staff*. The notes on each staff are determined by a symbol at the beginning of the staff called a *clef*. While there are many clefs, by far the most common one is the *treble clef*, and this is the one used for guitar music. The clef tells us what notes the lines and spaces represent. As shown below, the *lines* in this staff represent these notes, in ascending order: E, G, B, D, and F. You can use an acronym to help you remember these notes (like "Every Good Boy Deserves Fudge"). The notes on the *spaces* between each line are F, A, C, and E ("face") in ascending order. You can have notes above or below the staff, too. To add notes beyond the spaces above and below, we use short horizontal lines called *ledger lines*. Here are the notes on the staff:

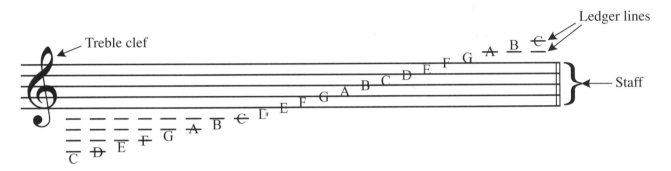

Music notation uses solid and hollow circles (technically, ovals) and lines to represent notes and their length. A hollow circle with no lines attached is a *whole note*, which gets four beats. A whole note fills a measure in 4/4 time, the most common *time signature* (see the later section on *Time Signatures* for more on this):

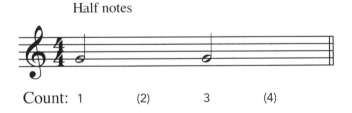

A hollow circle with a *stem* attached (the vertical line) is a *half note*, which gets two beats. Two half notes fit in each measure:

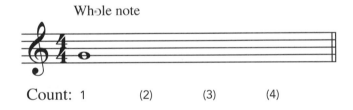

A solid circle with a stem attached is a *quarter note*, which gets one beat. There are four quarter notes in each measure:

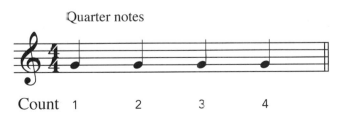

A solid circle that has a stem with a *flag* on it is an *eighth note*. On a single eighth note, a flag is a curvy line (shown below). When more than one eighth note is grouped together, their flags are often joined by *beams*. There are eight eighth notes in a measure:

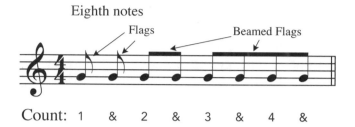

A solid circle that has a stem with a *double flag* is a *sixteenth note*. There are 16 sixteenth notes in a measure:

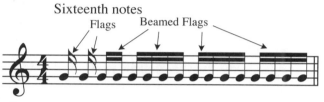

Time Signatures

Time signatures tell you what the rhythm is for a song, and they appear at the beginning of a piece, just after the *key signature* (which is explained in the next section). Time signatures look like a fraction—with two numbers stacked on top of each other. The top number tells you how many beats there are in each measure, and the bottom number tells you what the note value for each beat is. To get the correct beat value for the bottom number, you have to pretend it's the bottom number of a fraction where the number "1" would be on top. For instance, the following time signature—4/4— indicates four beats per measure and that a quarter note (1/4) gets a beat.

The most common time signature by far is 4/4, and you'll often see a "C" in place of the 4/4 marking; the "C" stands for "common time."

Waltzes and many other three-beat songs use the 3/4 time signature, which has three quarter note beats per measure:

In 6/8 time, there are six beats per measure, and one *eighth note* gets a beat:

In 6/8 time, however, the beats are often grouped into two sets of three notes. In this case, though there *are* six beats per measure, it's often counted *one*-and-ah, *two*-and-ah, instead of *one*-two-three *four*-five-six.

Key Signatures

Sharps and flats are referred to together as *accidentals*, and every key has its own set of accidentals that we call its *key signature*. The key signature is located at the beginning of a song and at the beginning of each new line of music. The following key signature has three sharps:

When sharps or flats appear in a key signature, every time a note is written on that line or space, you don't have to mark that it's a sharp or flat since that has been designated in the key signature. Because of this, key signatures make things easier to write. Of course, if there's a sharp in the key signature, and you want the note to *not* be played as a sharp note, you have to put a *natural* in front of the note. If you want the note sharped again in the same measure, you have to write out that sharp to counteract the previous natural:

In following measures, the key signature would apply again, and you wouldn't need to write out the sharp (though sometimes a *courtesy accidental* is still given as a reminder).

KEY SIGNATURES WITH FLATS

When flats occur in a key signature, they happen in the following order: B♭–E♭–A♭–D♭–G♭–C♭–F♭.

When your key signature has flats in it and you're playing in a *major* key, a quick way to know what key you are in is to look at the second-to-last flat. *That* is the key! For instance, when you have four flats (B♭, E♭, A♭, and D♭), the second-to-last flat is A♭, so you are in the key of A♭ major:

When you have just one flat, you're in the key of F major:

When your key signature has flats and you're in a minor key, a quick way to know what key you're in is to count up two whole steps from the last flat, and that note is the key (see more on *steps* and *intervals* in the following sections). For instance, when you have three flats, if you count up two whole steps from the last flat (A♭), you reach C; you're in the key of C minor:

If you have five flats, counting up two whole steps from the G♭, you reach B♭; you're in the key of B♭ minor.

KEY SIGNATURES WITH SHARPS

When sharps occur in a key signature, they appear in the following order: F♯–C♯–G♯–D♯–A♯–E♯–B♯. Notice how that's exactly *opposite* of the order that flats appear.

When your key signature has sharps in it and you're playing in a *major* key, a quick way to know what key you are in is to look at the last sharp and then move up one half step. For instance, when you have two sharps (F♯ and C♯), if you move up one half step from C♯, you reach D, which is the key:

When your key signature has sharps and you're in a minor key, a quick way to know what key you're in is to count down one whole step from the last sharp, and that note is the key. For instance, when you have two sharps, if you count down one whole step from the last sharp (C♯), you reach B; you're in the key of B minor:

If you have four sharps, counting down one whole step from the D♯, you reach C♯; you're in the key of C♯ minor.

Chord Theory

You don't need to know theory to play music, but it can help you understand the music you play better. If you'd like to learn more about chord-construction theory, read on!

TRIADS

Triad is a Greek word that means "three," and that's exactly what a triad contains—three notes! Triads are the most common type of chord. They are built by stacking two 3rds on top of each other. When we say "3rds," we're talking about *intervals*—the distances between notes. If you start on one note and move up the scale, the distance between the first note and the next note is a *2nd*. The distance between the first note and the third note is a *3rd*, between the first and fourth is a *4th*, and so on. A 3rd can be either major or minor, and stacking these 3rds on top of each other in different combinations creates four types of triads: major, minor, diminished, and augmented. Here is what's known as a C major triad:

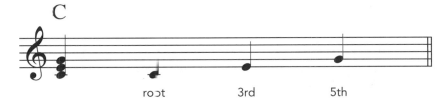

The defining note of a chord (its letter name) is called the *root*. Notice how the second note in the triad is the 3rd. The top note is called the 5th because its interval with the root is a 5th (count up yourself to see). After we take a closer look at intervals, we'll look at the different types of triads you can build with those intervals. So, continue on for more on triads.

INTERVALS

The *triad* section briefly discussed what an interval is: the distance between any two notes. Counting up from the first note to the second note will give you the interval between those two notes. That distance is quantified with a number, but intervals also have another component: their *quality*. The quality of any interval can be major, minor, diminished, augmented, or perfect. Looking at the twelve notes in a chromatic scale, along with their intervals, can help explain the differences between these qualities:

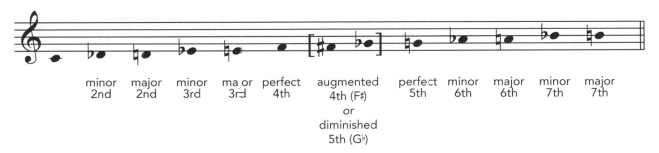

You may notice that every minor interval is one half step smaller than its major-interval counterpart. The only intervals that are not major or minor are the *perfect* intervals—the 4th and 5th. Lowering a perfect interval (like the 4th) results in a *diminished* interval, while raising a perfect interval (like the 5th) results in an *augmented* interval. All the other non-perfect intervals can be diminished or augmented as well, though it rarely happens. Here's how: if you lower a minor interval by one half step, it becomes diminished; and if you raise a major interval by one half step, it becomes augmented.

Now let's look at all the different types of triads we can build with these intervals. There are four types: major, minor, diminished, and augmented. Major triads have a major 3rd and a perfect 5th; minor triads have a minor 3rd and a perfect 5th; diminished triads have a minor 3rd and a diminished 5th; and augmented triads have a major 3rd and an augmented 5th:

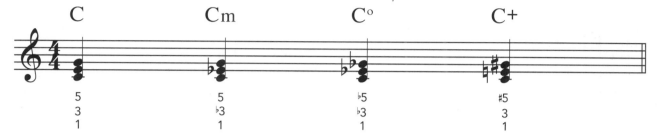

Major triads are labeled with just a letter (C), minor triads are labeled with a lowercase "m" (Cm), diminished triads are labelled with a "°" (C°), and augmented chords are labeled with a "+" (C+).

SEVENTH CHORDS

Seventh chords are four-note chords that stack a 7th interval on top of a triad. There are five types of unaltered seventh chords: dominant seventh (labeled with a "7" after the chord's letter name), minor seventh (m7), major seventh (maj7), minor-major seventh [m(maj7)], and diminished seventh (°7). Here are the seventh chords with a C root:

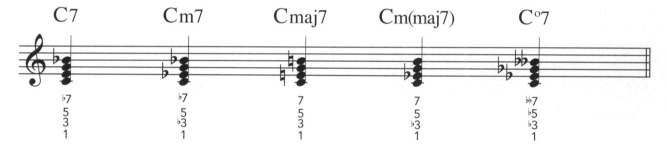

EXTENDED CHORDS

Beyond seventh chords, you can add further *extensions* to color the chord even more. Basically, you continue stacking 3rds on top of a seventh chord to build extended chords. Stack one 3rd on top, and you have a ninth chord; add a 3rd to the ninth chord, and you have an eleventh chord; and add a 3rd to that, and you get a thirteenth chord.

Not all notes of an extended chord are necessary to complete the chord. This is especially true on guitar, where a full thirteenth chord would be impossible to play, since you'd need to play seven notes and you only have six strings! But some of the notes are more important to include than others. For a chord to be an extended chord, you have to include the 7th and the extension. After that, including the 3rd, root, and other extensions, hold lesser priority. The least important note to include in an extended chord is the 5th.

It's also important to note that extensions can appear in a different octave than their numerical name implies. For instance, a 13th down one octave is a 6th. You can use that 6th (instead of a 13th) in your chord, and it will still be considered a 13th chord as long as you have a 7th in the chord as well.

SUSPENDED, "ADD," AND OTHER CHORDS

Suspended chords (sus) are formed when a note is substituted for a chord tone. In a sus4 chord, for instance, the 4th is substituted for the 3rd. "Add" chords are simply chords that add one or several notes to any particular chord. The difference between a sus4 and an add4 chord is that the sus4 does not include the 3rd, while the add4 does. Of course, like the English language, there are always a few exceptions. A triad with an added 6th is simply a sixth chord (though it could be written as an add6 chord), and a chord with the 6th and 9th added is simply called a "six-nine chord."

ALTERED CHORDS

Any chord can be altered, and that *alteration* is reflected in the chord's name. For instance, if you alter a seventh chord by lowering the 5th one half step, you have a 7♭5 chord; raise the 5th of that seventh chord by one half step, and you have a 7♯5 chord.

INVERSIONS

Any time that the lowest note in a chord is not the root, the chord is in *inversion*. The more notes you have in a chord, the more possible inversions you have. For instance, a seventh chord can be played in more inversions than a triad.

SAME SHAPES, DIFFERENT NAMES

Many chords can be called more than one name. For instance, a ♭5th is equivalent to a ♯11, and a chord containing one of these notes could be labeled either way. Likewise, a ♯5th and a ♭13th are also equivalent.

Chord Functions

Chord functions are numbers used to represent chords and their relationships to each other in a given key. To find the chord functions in any key, you need to understand the construction of the major and minor scales.

MAJOR SCALE AND MAJOR KEY CHORD FUNCTIONS

In major keys, the chords are all built from the corresponding major scale. To build a major scale, start on a note and move up with the following formula of whole steps and half steps: whole, whole, half, whole, whole, whole, half (a whole step is a two-fret distance, while a half step is a one-fret distance). Here is a C major scale with each step mapped out:

C Major Scale

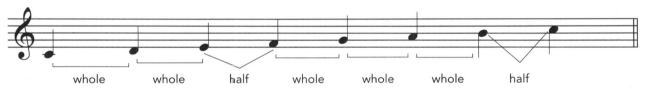

Every pair of notes has a sharp (or flat) note between them, *except* for two places: between B and C, and between E and F. When you use the major scale formula to build scales starting on notes other than C, the formula will include some (at least one) notes with sharps or flats. Here's the formula applied to a D note to build a D major scale:

D Major Scale

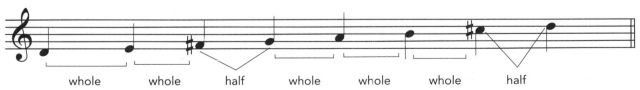

And here we'll build a G major scale:

G Major Scale

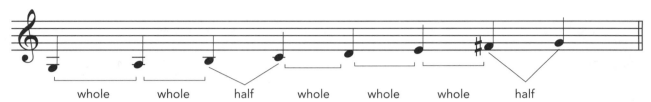

Once we know how to build a major scale, we can then build our chord functions. Let's go back to the C major scale, and we'll simply "build" chords from each scale degree by stacking notes on top of the scale in 3rds. To build a 3rd, simply start from the note you're on, skip a note, and add the next note up. So, to add a 3rd on top of C, you'd skip D and add an E. To add a 3rd on top of that, skip F and add G. Each chord is built from two 3rds stacked on top of each other. Here is the C major scale with 3rds stacked on top of it, or the *harmonized C major scale*:

Chord Functions (from Harmonized Major Scale)

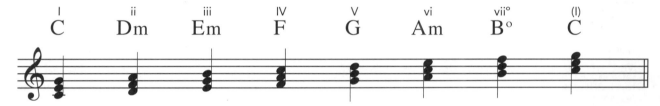

Each one of these chords gets a number that corresponds to its degree. Major chords are upper-case, and minor chords are lowercase. The vii° chord is diminished, and we won't worry about that one since it's rarely used. Instead, a ♭VII chord is often used. This simply shifts the bottom note of the chord down a half step (one fret):

This set of chord functions holds the same relationships for all major keys, so to find the chord functions for any other key, first build a major scale, then harmonize it with 3rds, and you have your chord functions in that key. For instance, to find the chord functions in the key of G major, first build a G major scale:

G Major Scale

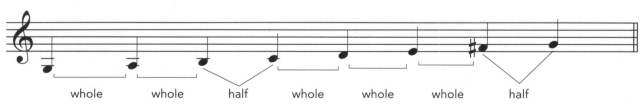

Next, harmonize the scale in 3rds. Here are the major chord functions for G major:

Chord Functions for G Major

MINOR SCALE AND MINOR KEY CHORD FUNCTIONS

To build a minor scale, we use the following whole- and half-step formula: whole, half, whole, whole, half, whole, whole. Here's an Am scale:

A Minor Scale

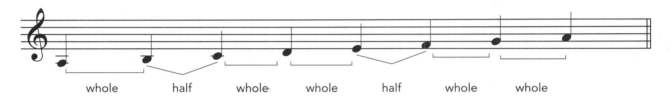

Stacking 3rds gives us the following chord functions for the Am scale:

A Minor Chord Functions (from Harmonized Minor Scale)

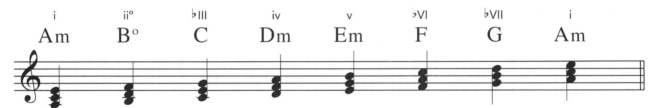

This minor key set of chords holds the same relationship for all minor keys. To find the chord functions in another key, first build the minor scale affiliated with that key, then harmonize the scale to find the chord functions. For instance, to find the chord functions in Em, first build an Em scale:

E Minor Scale

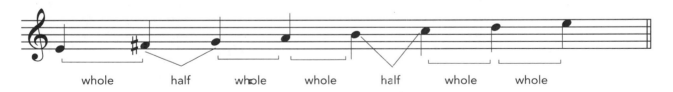

Then harmonize the scale with 3rds and you have your chord functions for Em:

Chord Functions for E Minor

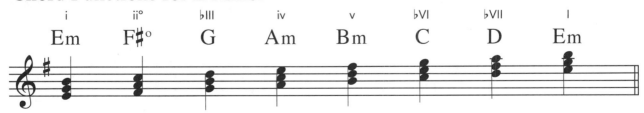

HAL LEONARD GUITAR METHOD

by Will Schmid and Greg Koch

THE HAL LEONARD GUITAR METHOD is designed for anyone just learning to play acoustic or electric guitar. It is based on years of teaching guitar students of all ages, and it also reflects some of the best guitar teaching ideas from around the world. This comprehensive method includes: A learning sequence carefully paced with clear instructions; popular songs which increase the incentive to learn to play; versatility – can be used as self-instruction or with a teacher; audio accompaniments so that students have fun and sound great while practicing.

BOOK 1
00699010 Book $6.99
00699027 Book/CD Pack $10.99

BOOK 2
00699020 Book $6.99
00697313 Book/CD Pack $9.99

BOOK 3
00699030 Book $6.99
00697316 Book/CD Pack $9.95

COMPOSITE
Books 1, 2, and 3 bound together in an easy-to-use spiral binding.
00699040 Books Only $14.99
00697342 Book/3-CD Pack $24.99

DVD
FOR THE BEGINNING ELECTRIC OR ACOUSTIC GUITARIST
00697318 DVD $19.95
00697341 Book/CD Pack and DVD $24.99

GUITAR FOR KIDS
A BEGINNER'S GUIDE WITH STEP-BY-STEP INSTRUCTION FOR ACOUSTIC AND ELECTRIC GUITAR
by Bob Morris and Jeff Schroedl
00865003 Book/CD Pack $12.99
00697402 Songbook Book/CD Pack $9.99

SONGBOOKS

EASY POP MELODIES
00697281 Book $6.99
00697268 Book/CD Pack $14.99

MORE EASY POP MELODIES
00697280 Book $6.99
00697269 Book/CD Pack $14.99

EVEN MORE EASY POP MELODIES
00699154 Book $6.95
00697270 Book/CD Pack $14.99

EASY POP RHYTHMS
00697336 Book $6.95
00697309 Book/CD Pack $14.99

MORE EASY POP RHYTHMS
00697338 Book $6.95
00697322 Book/CD Pack $14.95

EVEN MORE EASY POP RHYTHMS
00697340 Book $6.95
00697323 Book/CD Pack $14.95

EASY SOLO GUITAR PIECES
00110407 Book $9.99

EASY POP CHRISTMAS MELODIES
00697417 Book $6.99
00697416 Book/CD Pack $14.99

LEAD LICKS
00697345 Book/CD Pack...........................$9.99

RHYTHM RIFFS
00697346 Book/CD Pack...........................$9.95

STYLISTIC METHODS

ACOUSTIC GUITAR
00697347 Book/CD Pack $16.95
00697384 Acoustic Guitar Songs $14.95

BLUEGRASS GUITAR
00697405 Book/CD Pack $16.99

BLUES GUITAR
00697326 Book/CD Pack $16.99
00697385 Blues Guitar Songs $14.95

BRAZILIAN GUITAR
00697415 Book/CD Pack $14.99

CHRISTIAN GUITAR
00695947 Book/CD Pack $12.99
00697408 Christian Guitar Songs............$14.99

CLASSICAL GUITAR
00697376 Book/CD Pack $14.99
00697388 Classical Guitar Pieces $9.99

COUNTRY GUITAR
00697337 Book/CD Pack $22.99
00697400 Country Guitar Songs $14.99

FINGERSTYLE GUITAR
00697378 Book/CD Pack $17.99
00697432 Fingerstyle Guitar Songs $14.99

FLAMENCO GUITAR
00697363 Book/CD Pack $14.99

FOLK GUITAR
00697414 Book/CD Pack $14.99

JAZZ GUITAR
00695359 Book/CD Pack $19.99
00697386 Jazz Guitar Songs $14.95

JAZZ-ROCK FUSION
00697387 Book/CD Pack $19.99

ROCK GUITAR
00697319 Book/CD Pack $16.95
00697383 Rock Guitar Songs $14.95

ROCKABILLY GUITAR
00697407 Book/CD Pack $16.95

R&B GUITAR
00697356 Book/CD Pack $14.95
00697433 R&B Guitar Songs...................$14.95

REFERENCE

ARPEGGIO FINDER
00697352 6" x 9" Edition $5.99
00697351 9" x 12" Edition $6.99

INCREDIBLE CHORD FINDER
00697200 6" x 9" Edition $5.99
00697208 9" x 12" Edition $6.99

INCREDIBLE SCALE FINDER
00695568 6" x 9" Edition $5.99
00695490 9" x 12" Edition $6.99

GUITAR CHORD, SCALE & ARPEGGIO FINDER
00697410...$19.99

GUITAR SETUP & MAINTENANCE
00697427 6" X 9" Edition $14.99
00697421 9" X 12" Edition $12.99

GUITAR TECHNIQUES
00697389 Book/CD Pack $12.95

GUITAR PRACTICE PLANNER
00697401 ....$5.99

MUSIC THEORY FOR GUITARISTS
00695790 Book/CD Pack $19.99

HAL•LEONARD® CORPORATION

7777 W. BLUEMOUND RD. P.O. BOX 13819 MILWAUKEE, WI 53213

www.halleonard.com

Prices, contents and availability subject to change without notice.